FOR ORGANS, PIANOS & ELECTRONIC KEYBOARDS

91

2ND EDITION

THIRTY SONGS FOR A BETTER WORLD

T0210285

ISBN 978-0-7935-6958-8

CORPORATION

7777 W. BLUEMOUND RD. P.O. BOX 13819 MILWAUKEE, WI 53213

Visit Hal Leonard Online at
www.halleonard.com

CONTENTS

All You Need Is Love

Registration 5
Rhythm: Shuffle or Swing

Words and Music by John Lennon
and Paul McCartney

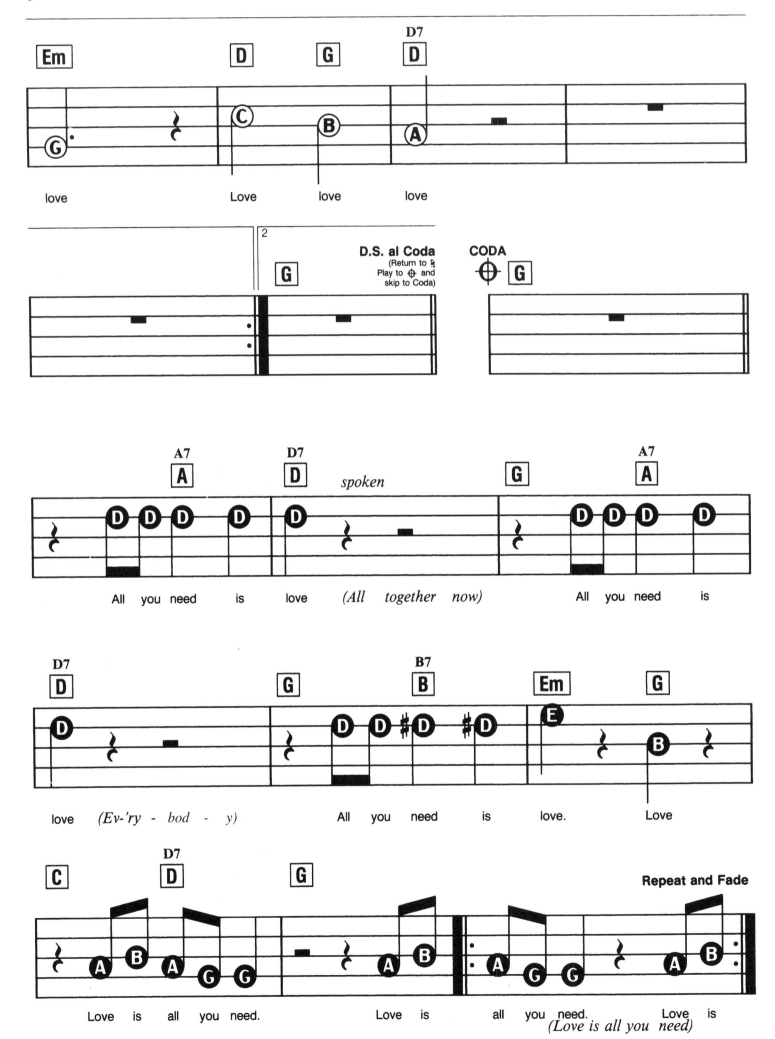

Candle on the Water
from Walt Disney's PETE'S DRAGON

Registration 1
Rhythm: Fox Trot or Ballad

Words and Music by Al Kasha
and Joel Hirschhorn

Bless the Beasts and Children
from BLESS THE BEASTS AND CHILDREN

Registration 3
Rhythm: Slow Rock or Ballad

Words and Music by Barry DeVorzon
and Perry Botkin, Jr.

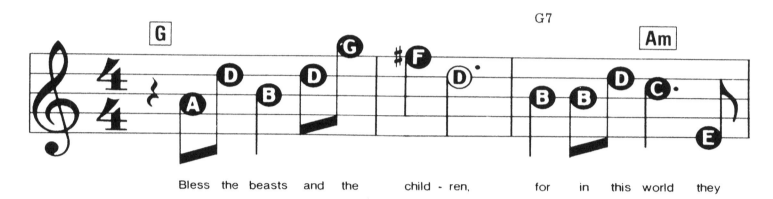

Bless the beasts and the child - ren, for in this world they

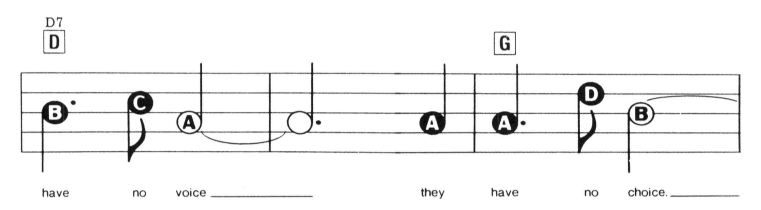

have no voice _____ they have no choice. _____

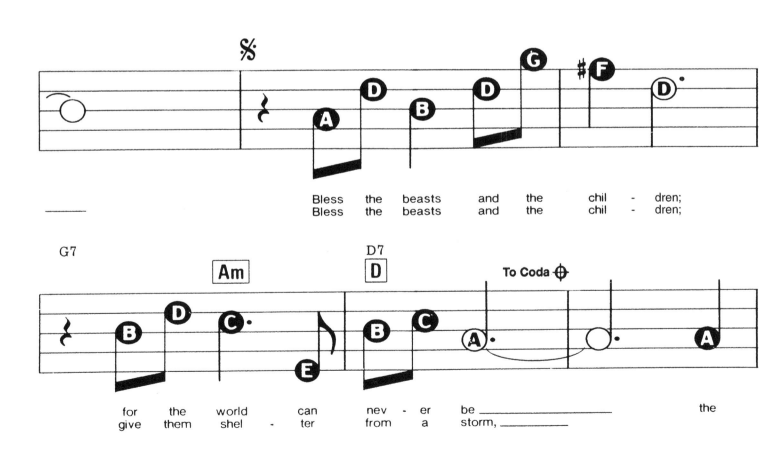

Bless the beasts and the chil - dren;
Bless the beasts and the chil - dren;

for the world can nev - er be _____ the
give them shel - ter from a storm, _____

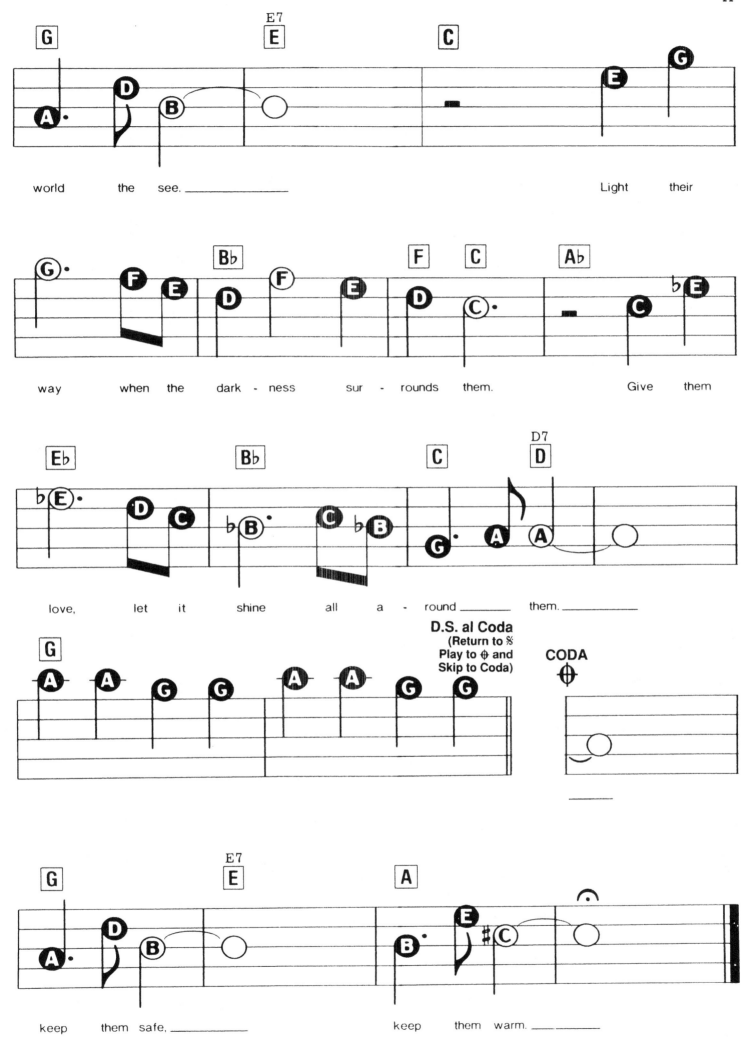

Change the World

Registration 7
Rhythm: Pop

Words and Music by Wayne Kirkpatrick,
Gordon Kennedy and Tommy Sims

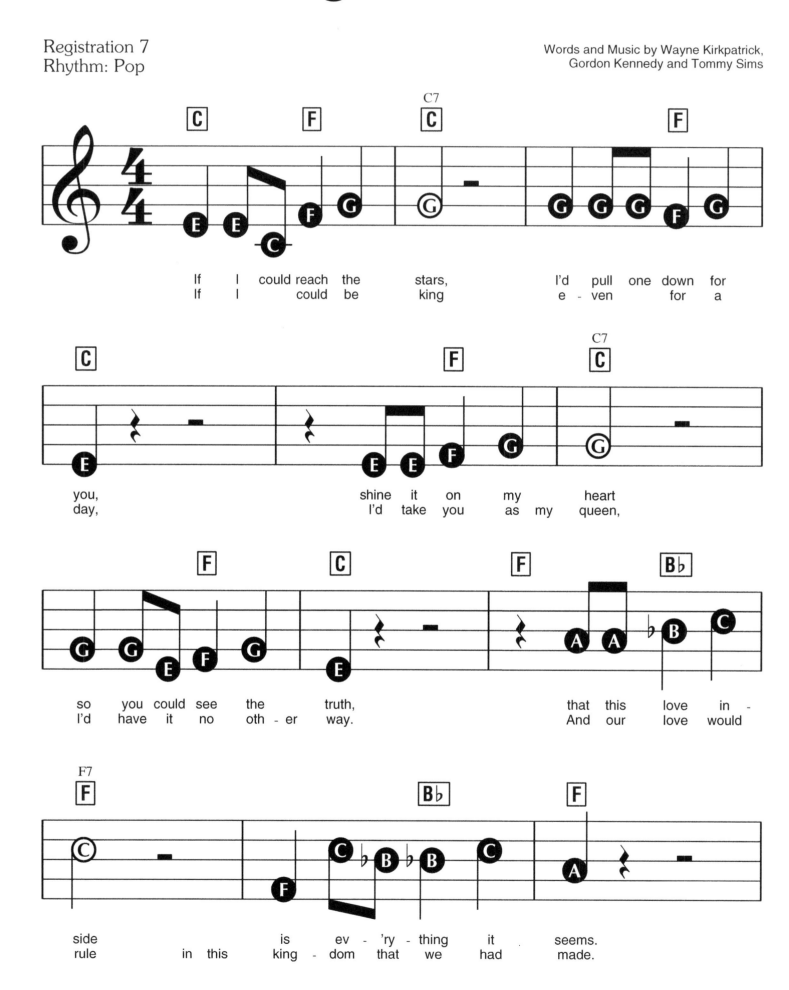

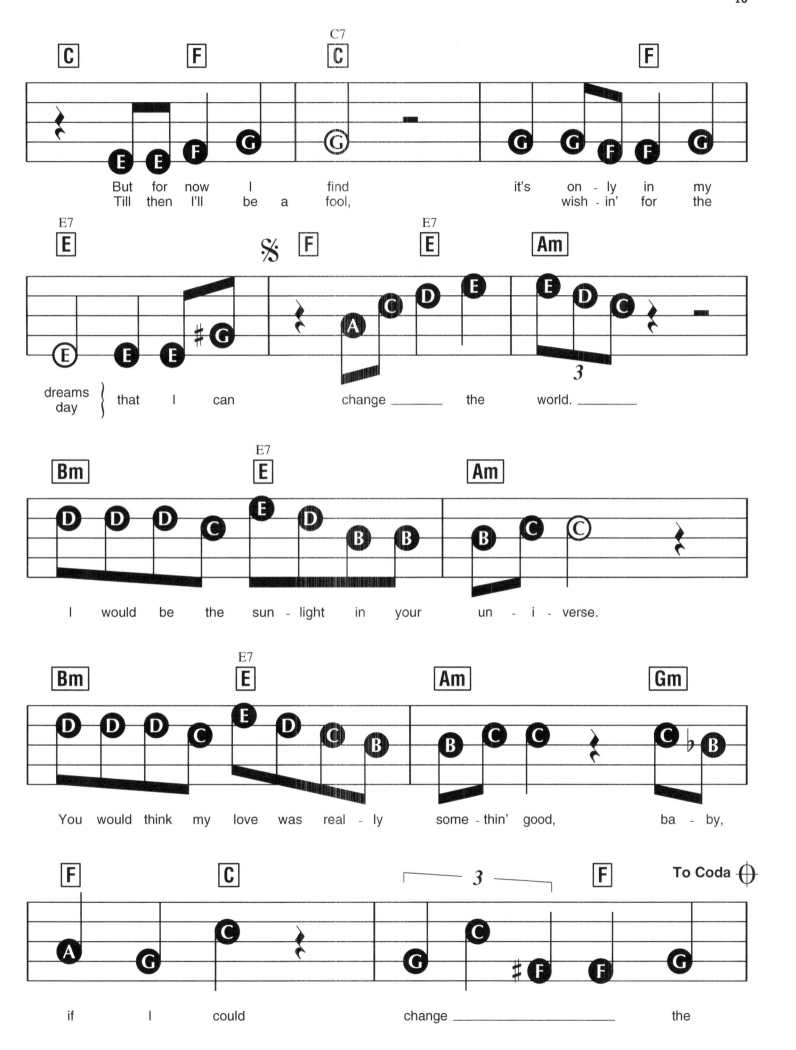

14

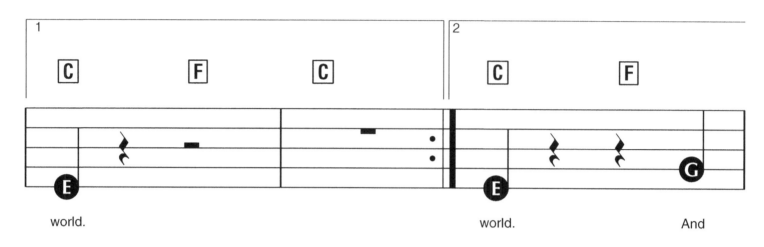

world.   world.   And

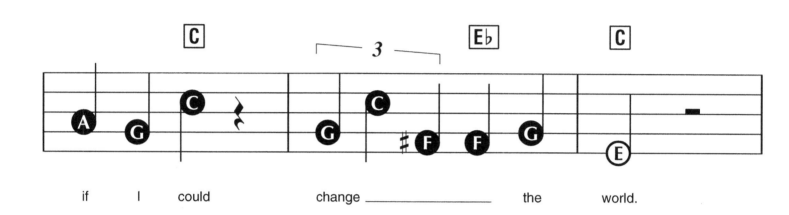

if   I   could   change &rule   the   world.

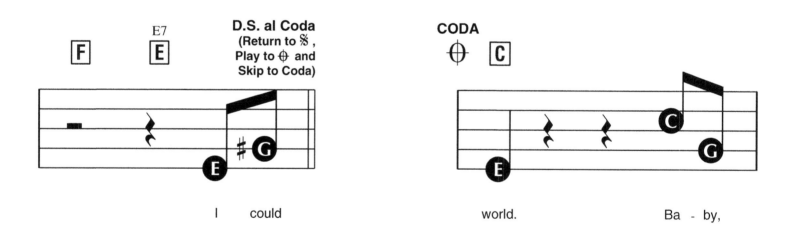

I   could   world.   Ba - by,

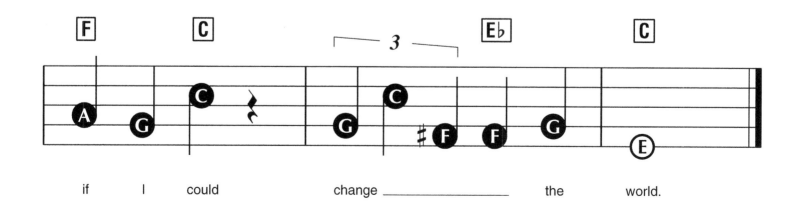

if   I   could   change &rule   the   world.

Circle of Life
from Walt Disney Pictures' THE LION KING

Registration 2
Rhythm: Calypso or Reggae

Music by Elton John
Lyrics by Tim Rice

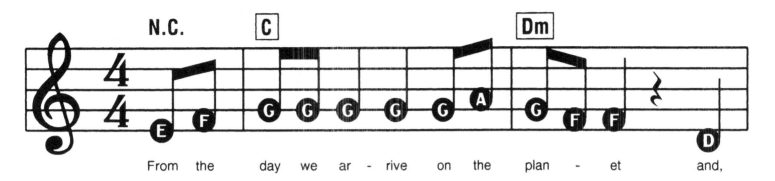

From the day we ar - rive on the plan - et and,

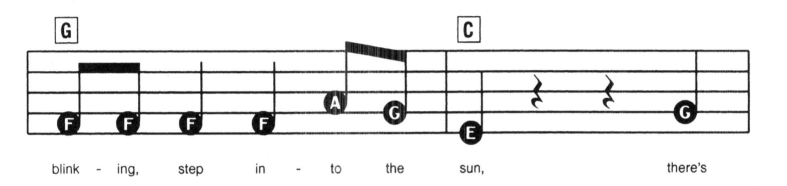

blink - ing, step in - to the sun, there's

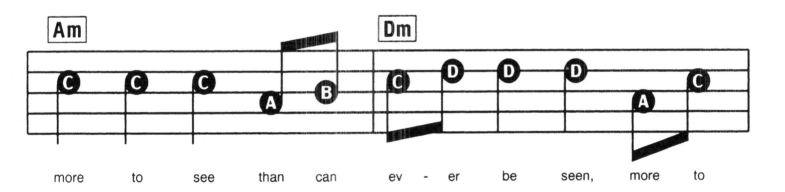

more to see than can ev - er be seen, more to

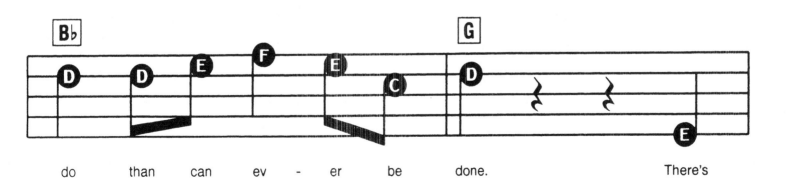

do than can ev - er be done. There's

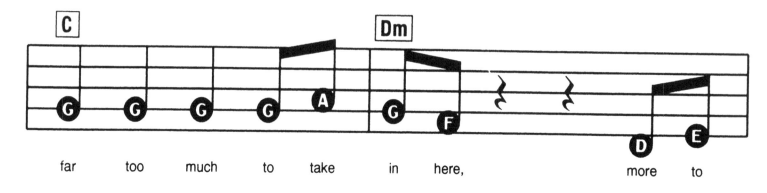

far   too   much   to   take   in   here,   more   to

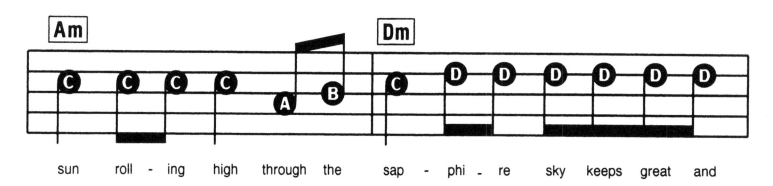

find   than   can   ev - er   be   found.   But   the

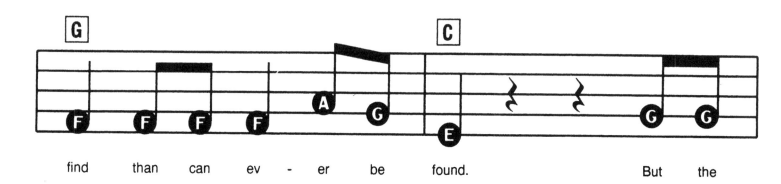

sun   roll - ing   high   through   the   sap - phi - re   sky   keeps   great   and

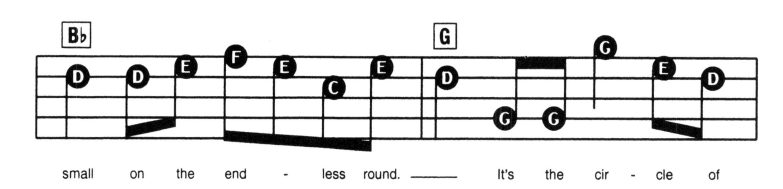

small   on   the   end - less   round. _____   It's   the   cir - cle   of

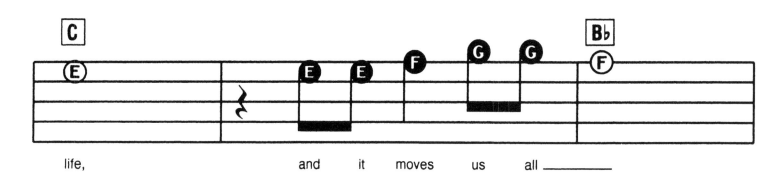

life,   and   it   moves   us   all _____

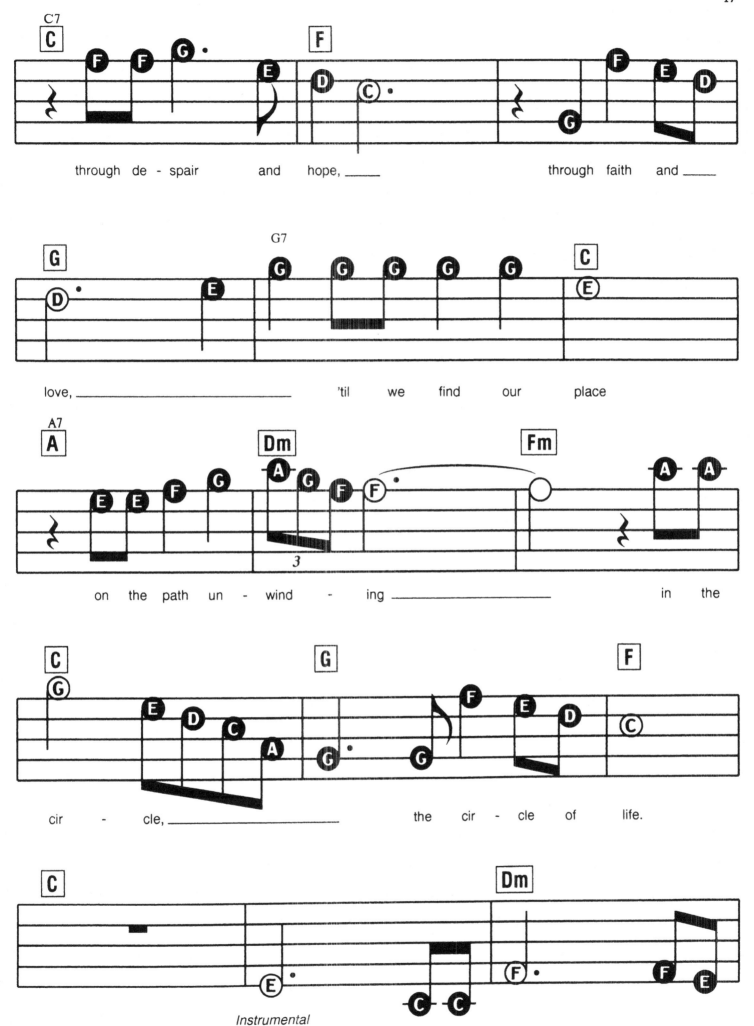

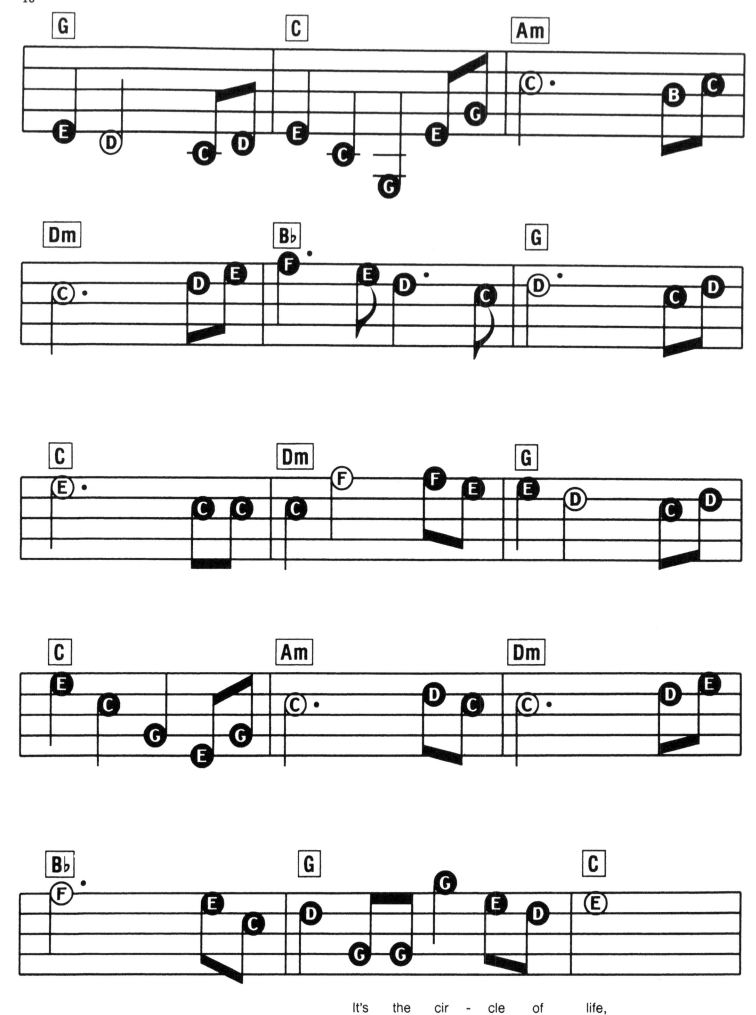

It's the cir - cle of life,

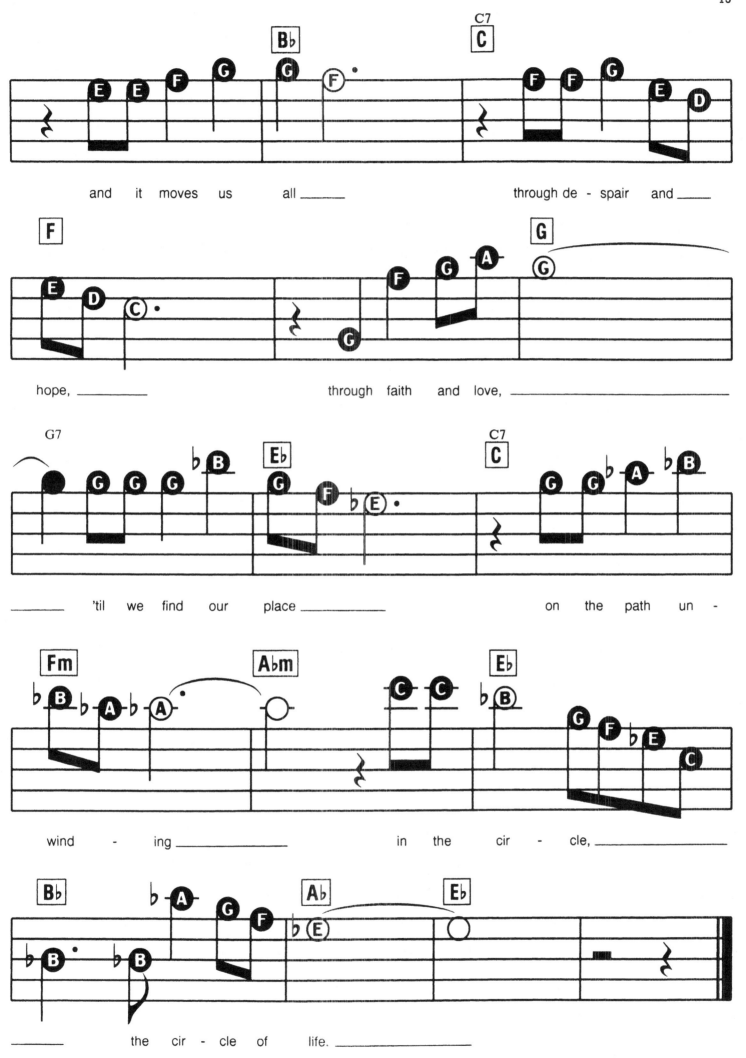

Colors of the Wind
from Walt Disney's POCAHONTAS

Registration 5
Rhythm: None

Music by Alan Menken
Lyrics by Stephen Schwartz

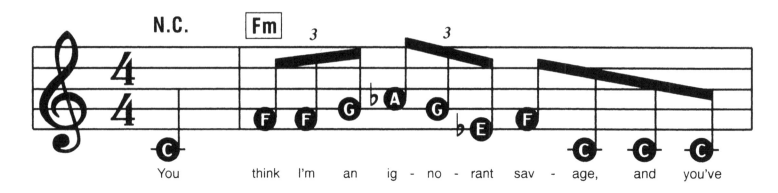

You think I'm an ig - no - rant sav - age, and you've

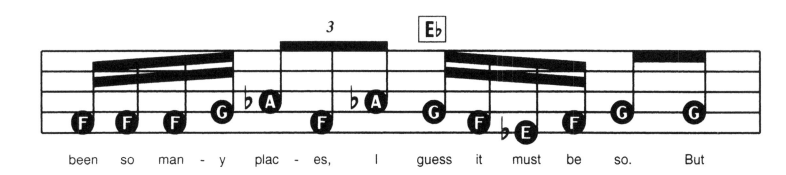

been so man - y plac - es, I guess it must be so. But

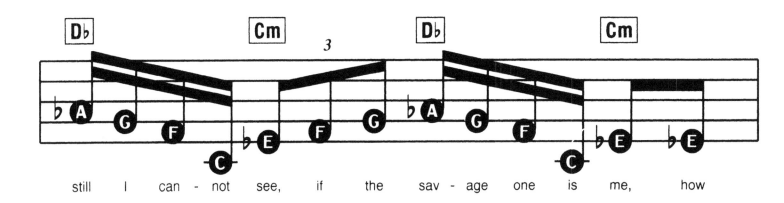

still I can - not see, if the sav - age one is me, how

Rhythm: Rock or 8 Beat

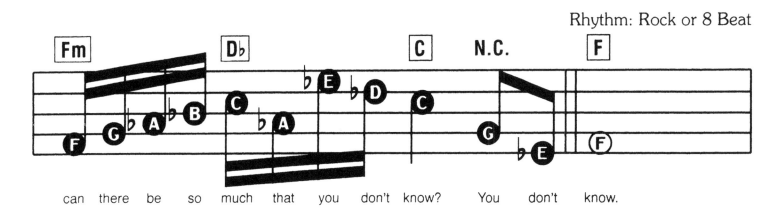

can there be so much that you don't know? You don't know.

22

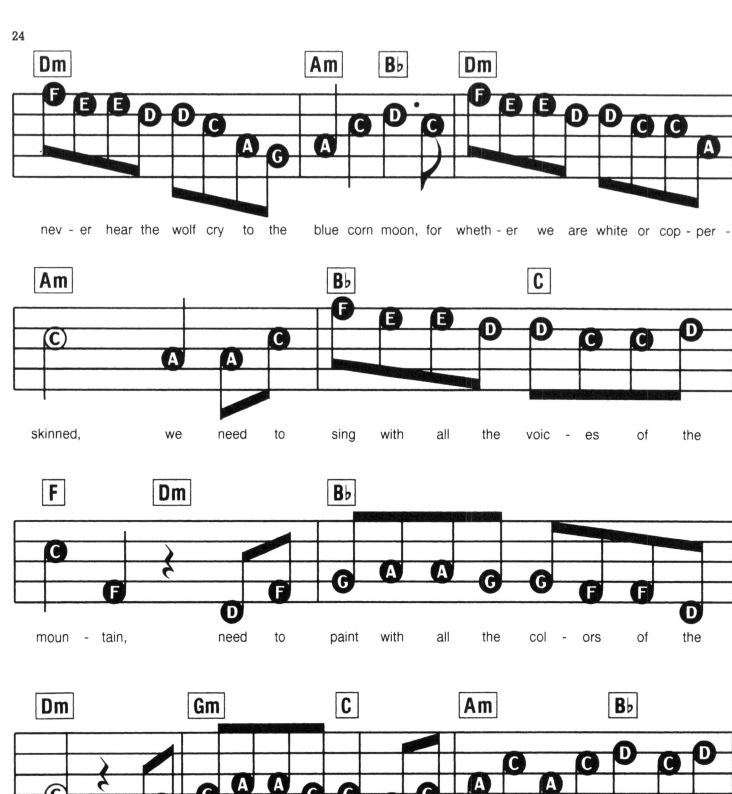

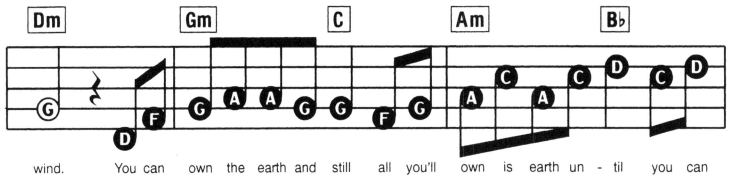

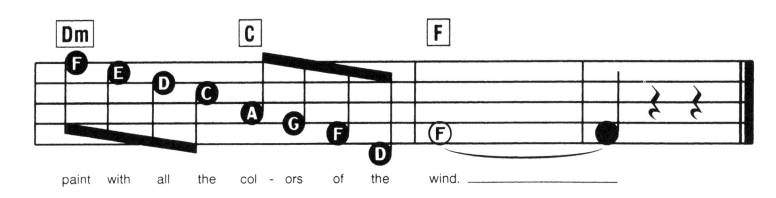

Count Your Blessings Instead of Sheep

from the Motion Picture Irving Berlin's WHITE CHRISTMAS

Registration 4
Rhythm: Swing

Words and Music by
Irving Berlin

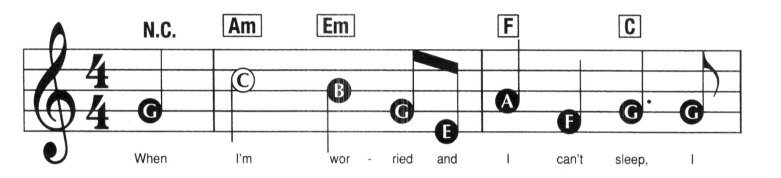

When I'm wor - ried and I can't sleep, I

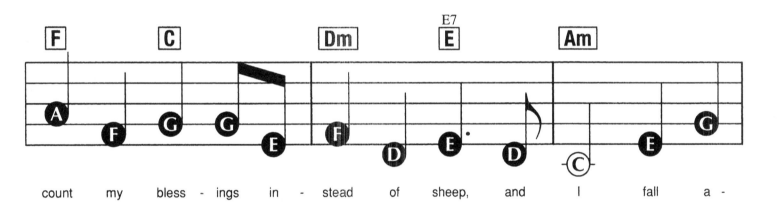

count my bless - ings in - stead of sheep, and I fall a -

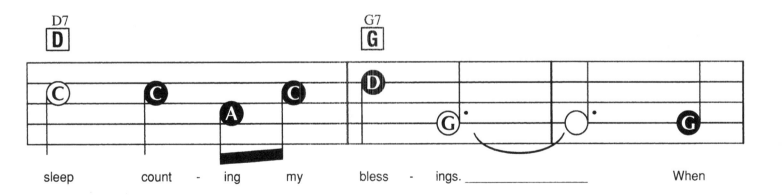

sleep count - ing my bless - ings. _____ When

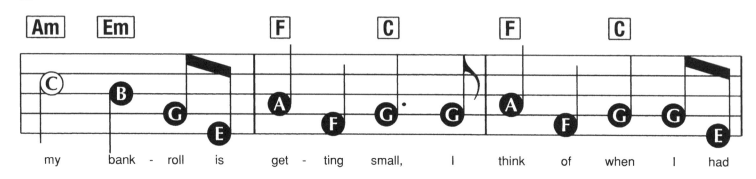

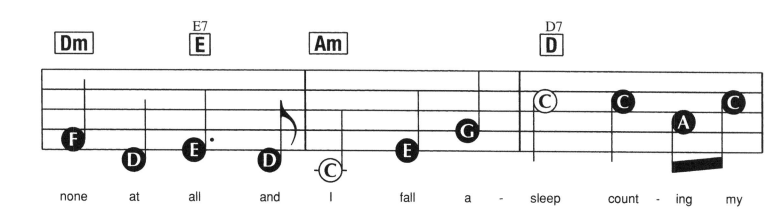

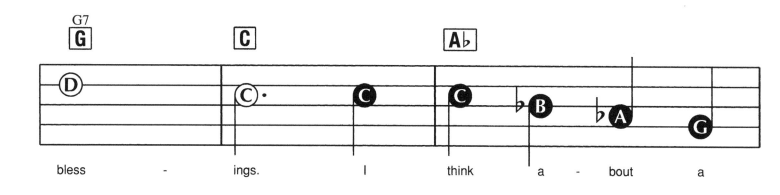

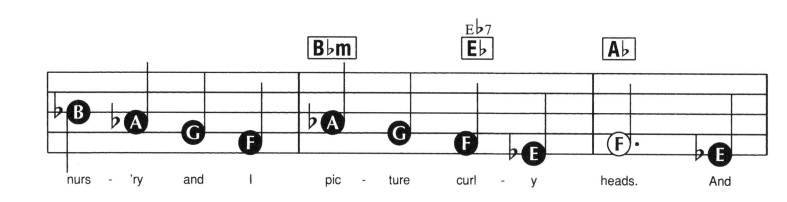

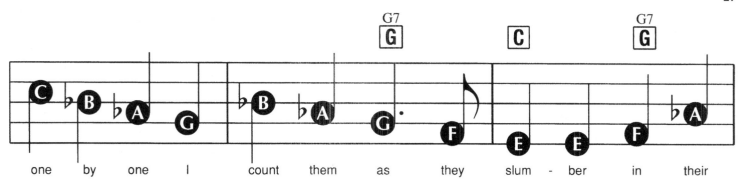

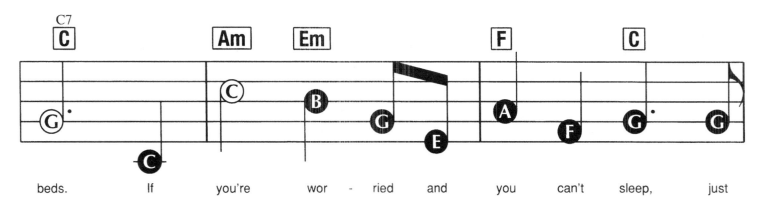

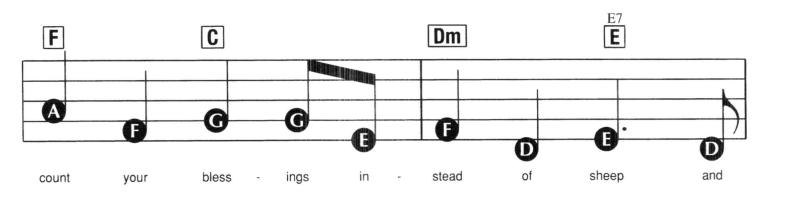

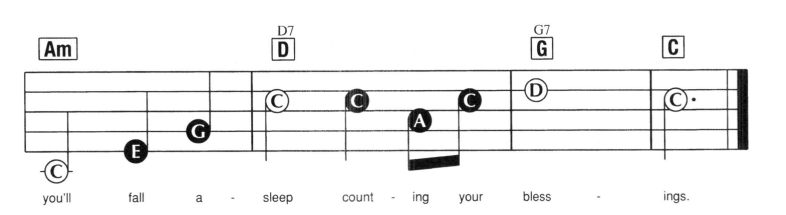

Everything Is Beautiful

Registration 8
Rhythm: Rock or Jazz Rock

Words and Music by
Ray Stevens

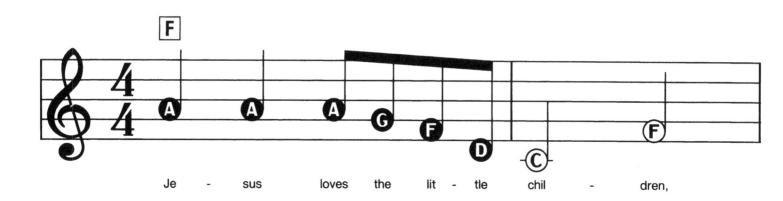

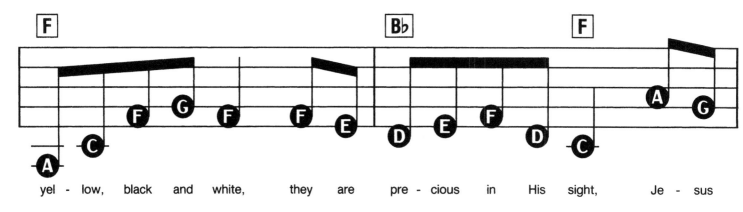

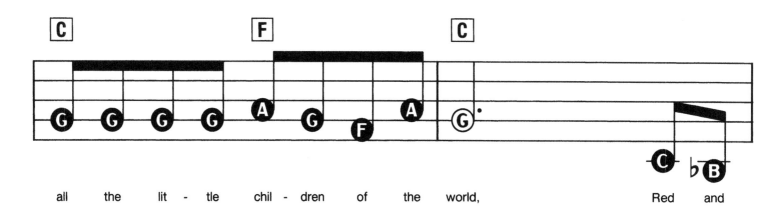

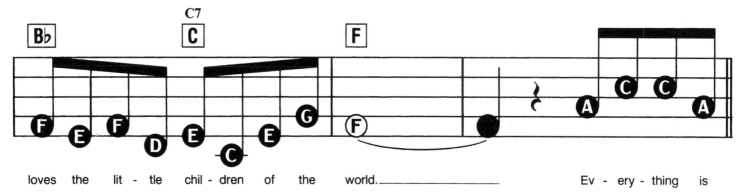

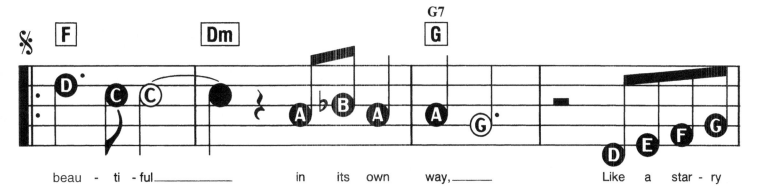

beau - ti - ful_____ in its own way,_____ Like a star - ry

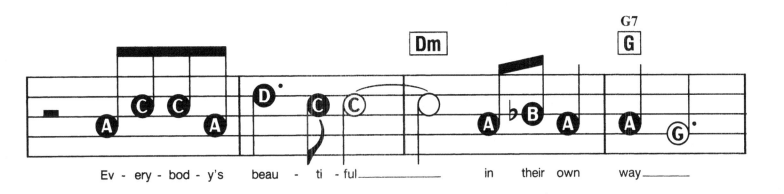

sum - mer night, or a snow - cov - ered win - ter's day.

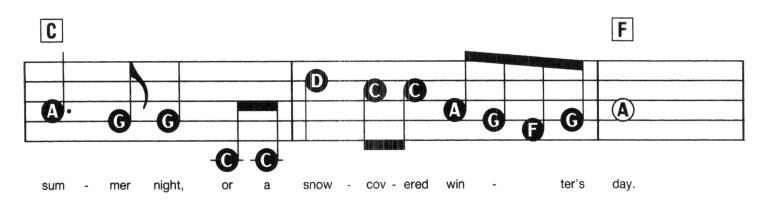

Ev - ery - bod - y's beau - ti - ful_____ in their own way_____

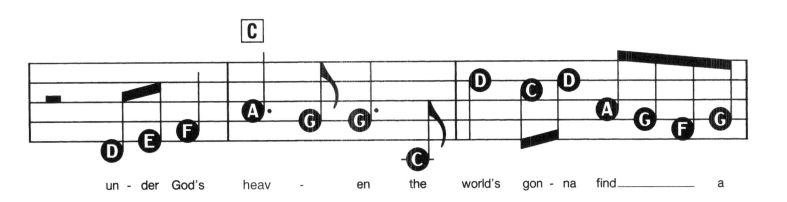

un - der God's heav - en the world's gon - na find_____ a

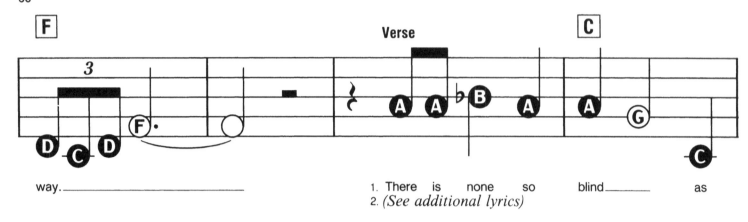

way._____

1. There is none so blind_____ as
2. *(See additional lyrics)*

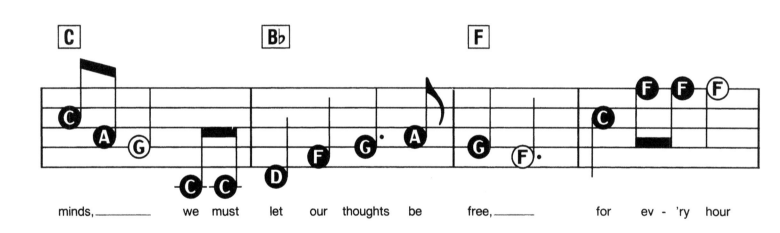

he   who   will   not   see,_____   We   must   not   close   our

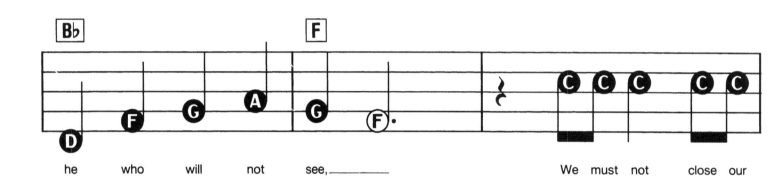

minds,_____   we   must   let   our   thoughts   be   free,_____   for   ev - 'ry   hour

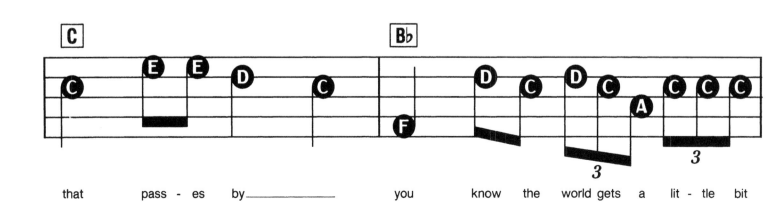

that   pass - es   by_____   you   know   the   world   gets   a   lit - tle   bit

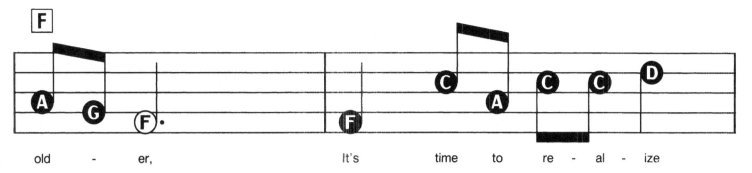

old - er,   It's   time   to   re - al - ize

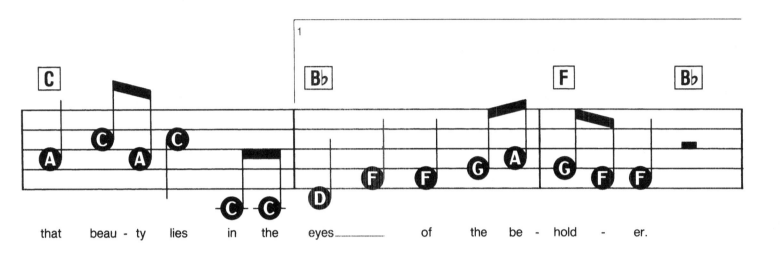

that   beau - ty   lies   in   the   eyes_____   of   the   be - hold   -   er.

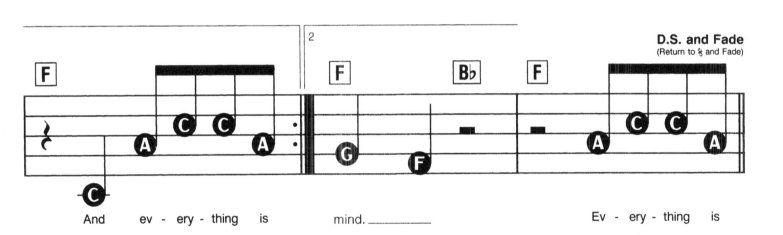

D.S. and Fade
(Return to 𝄋 and Fade)

And   ev - ery - thing   is   mind. _____   Ev - ery - thing   is

Additional Lyrics

2. We shouldn't care about the length of his hair or the color of his skin,
   Don't worry about what shows from without but the love that lives within,
   We gonna get it all together now and everything gonna work out fine,
   Just take a little time to look on the good side my friend and straighten it out in your mind.

Friends

Registration 4
Rhythm: Rock

Words and Music by Michael W. Smith
and Deborah D. Smith

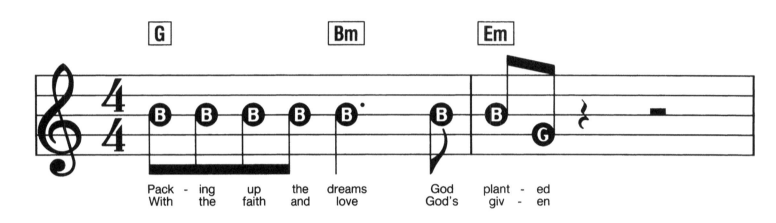

Pack - ing up the dreams God plant - ed
With the faith and love God's giv - en

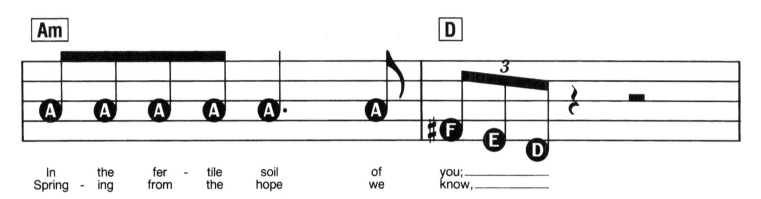

In the fer - tile soil of you;_____
Spring - ing from the hope we know,_____

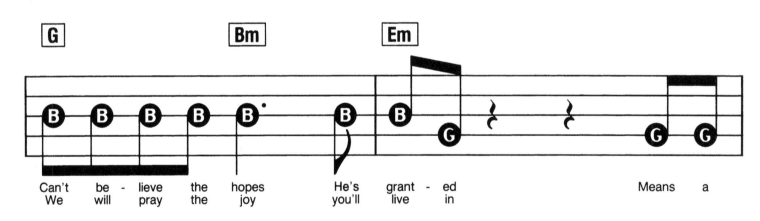

Can't be - lieve the hopes He's grant - ed   Means a
We will pray the joy you'll live in

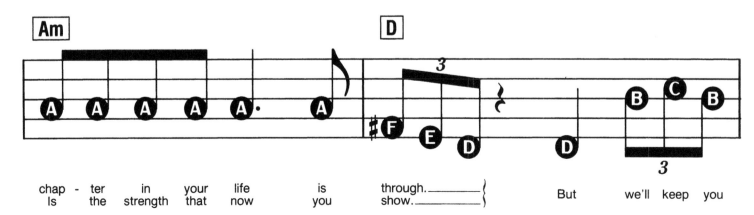

chap - ter in your life is through._____   But we'll keep you
Is the strength that now you show._____

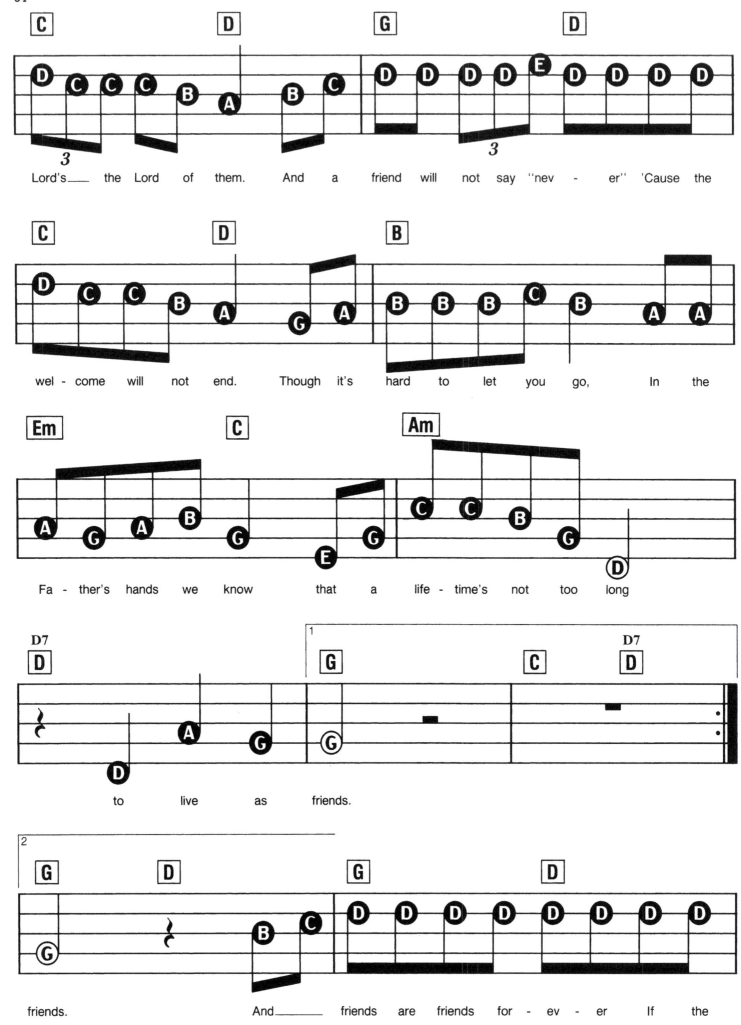

From a Distance

Registration 7
Rhythm: 8 Beat or Pops

Words and Music by
Julie Gold

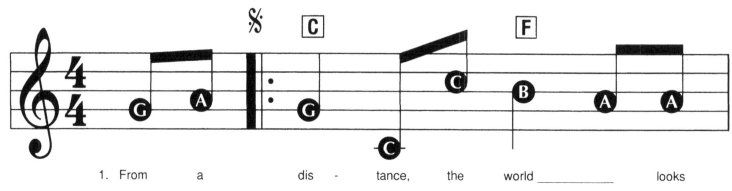

1. From   a   dis - tance,   the   world _____ looks

2., 3. *(See Additional Lyrics)*

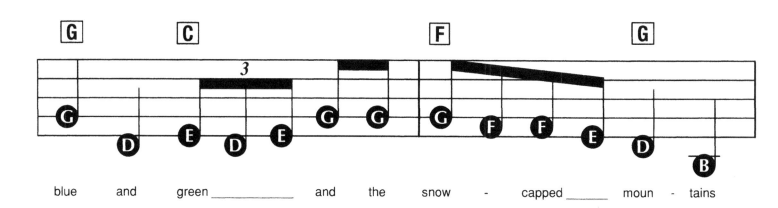

blue   and   green _____ and   the   snow - capped _____ moun - tains

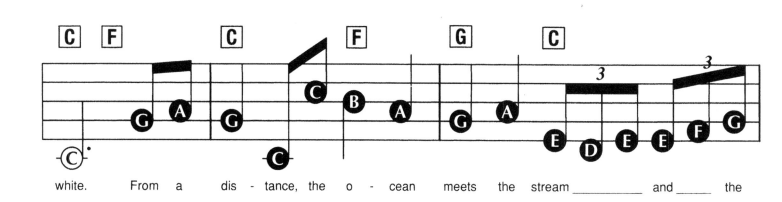

white.   From   a   dis - tance, the   o - cean   meets   the   stream _____ and _____ the

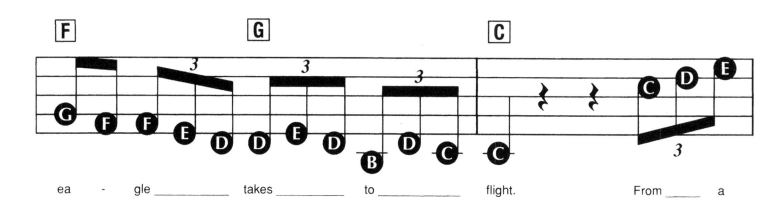

ea - gle _____ takes _____ to _____ flight.   From _____ a

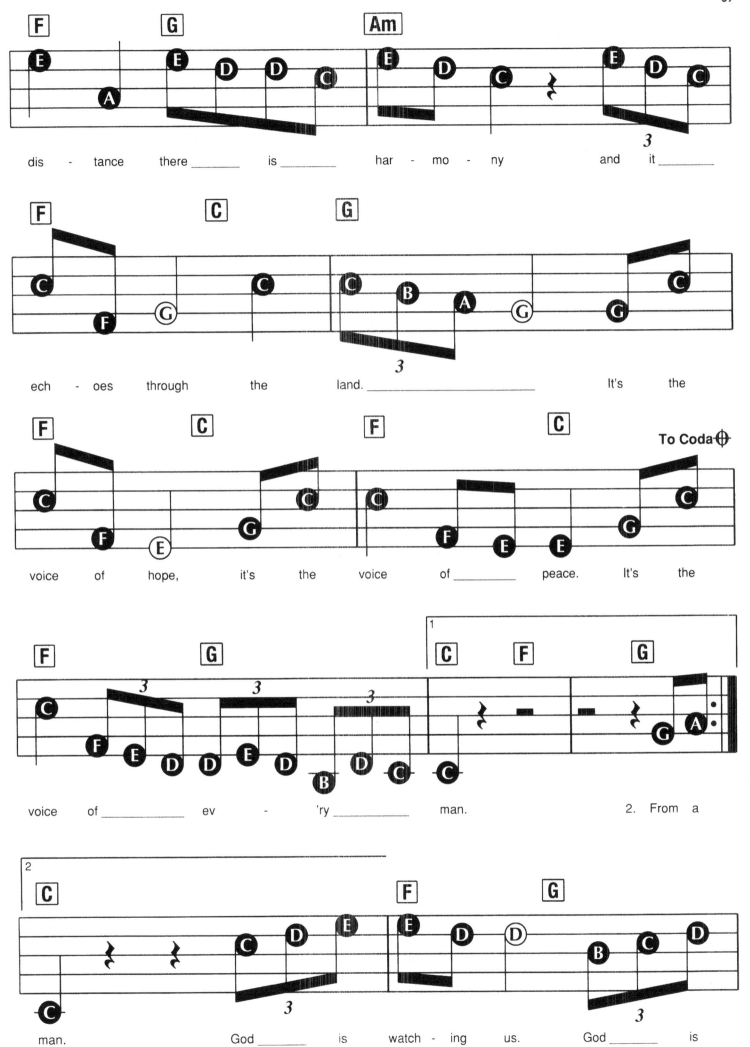

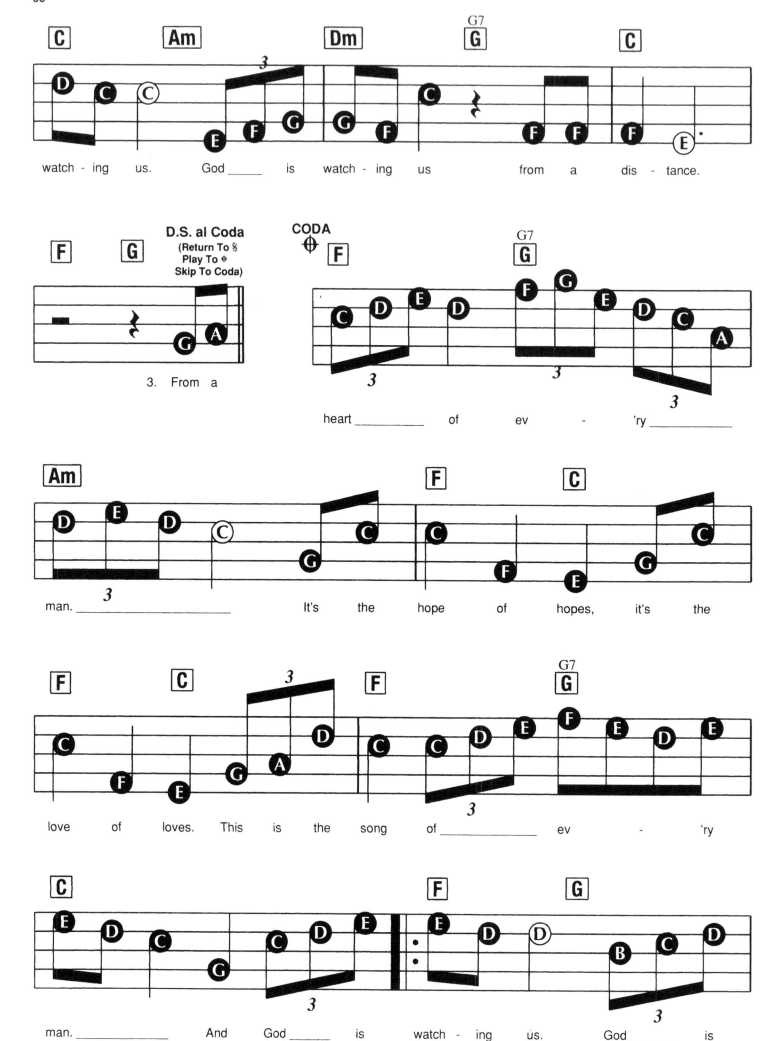

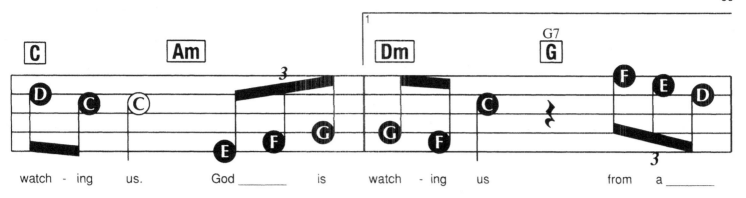

watch - ing us. God_____ is watch - ing us from a_____

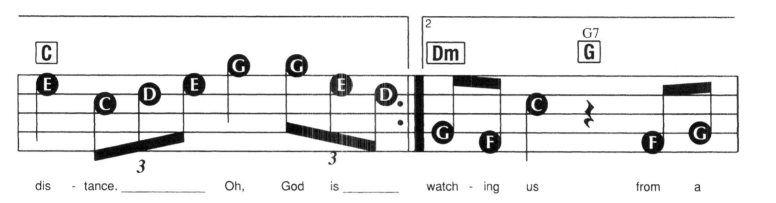

dis - tance._____ Oh, God is_____ watch - ing us from a

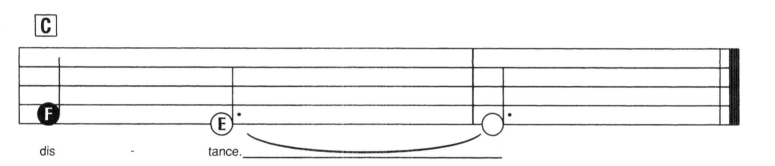

dis - tance._____

Additional Lyrics

2. From a distance, we all have enough,
   And no one is in need.
   There are no guns, no bombs, no diseases,
   No hungry mouths to feed.
   From a distance, we are instruments
   Marching in a common band;
   Playing songs of hope, playing songs of peace,
   They're the songs of every man.

3. From a distance, you look like my friend
   Even though we are at war.
   From a distance I just cannot comprehend
   What all this fighting is for.
   From a distance there is harmony
   And it echoes through the land.
   It's the hope of hopes, it's the love of loves.
   It's the heart of every man.

Gonna Build a Mountain
from the Musical Production STOP THE WORLD – I WANT TO GET OFF

Registration 4
Rhythm: Fox Trot

Words and Music by Leslie Bricusse
and Anthony Newley

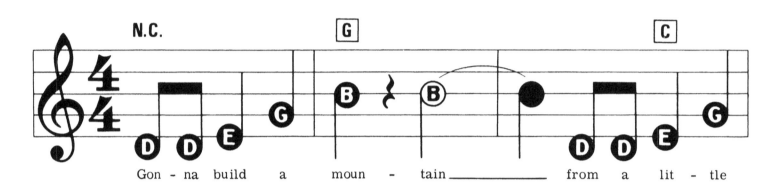

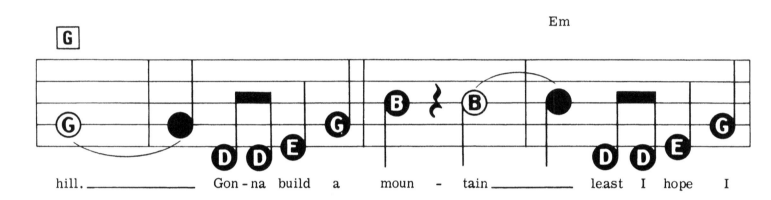

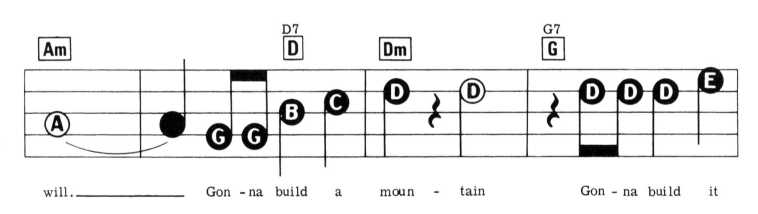

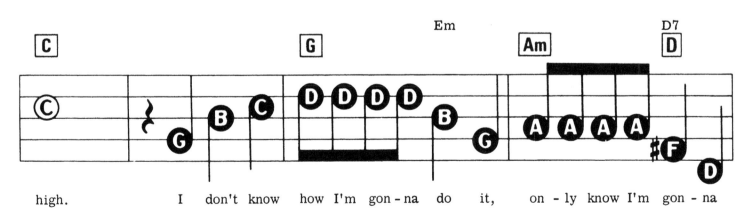

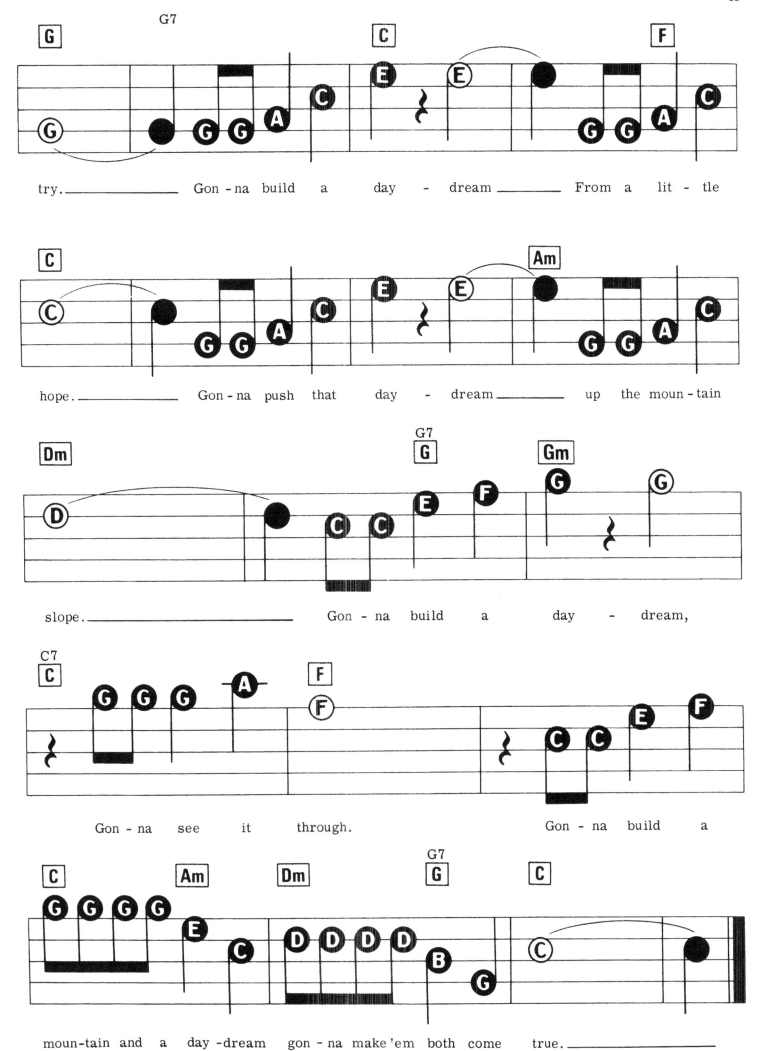

If I Had a Hammer
(The Hammer Song)

Registration 5
Rhythm: Rock or Fox Trot

Words and Music by Lee Hays
and Pete Seeger

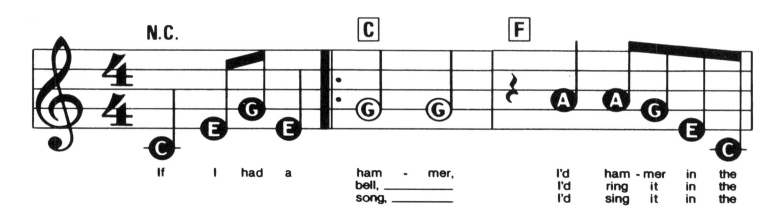

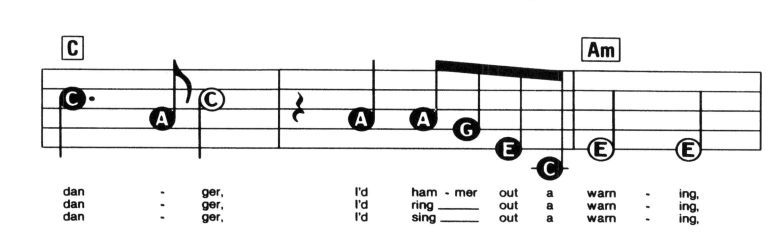

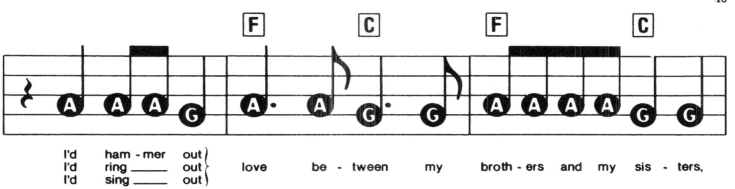

| F | C | F | C |

I'd ham-mer out
I'd ring _____ out
I'd sing _____ out
love be - tween my broth - ers and my sis - ters,

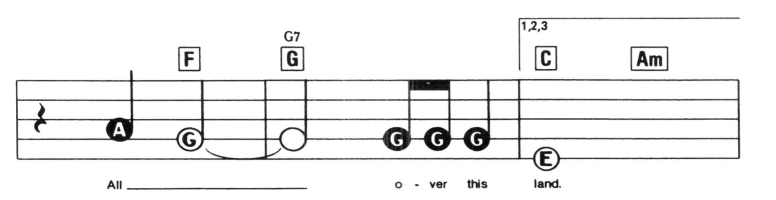

| F | G7 / G | 1,2,3 C | Am |

All _____ o - ver this land.

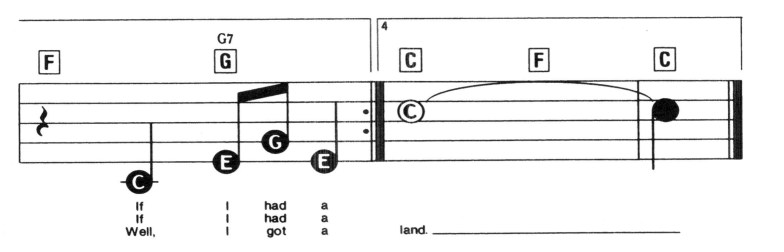

| F | G7 / G | 4 C | F | C |

If I had a
If I had a
Well, I got a
land. _____

Additional Verse

Well, I got a hammer,
And I've got a bell,
And I've got a song to sing,
All over this land;
It's the hammer of justice,
It's the bell of freedom,
It's the song about love between my brothers and my sisters,
All over this land.

If I Ruled the World
from PICKWICK

Registration 3
Rhythm: Swing

Words by Leslie Bricusse
Music by Cyril Ornadel

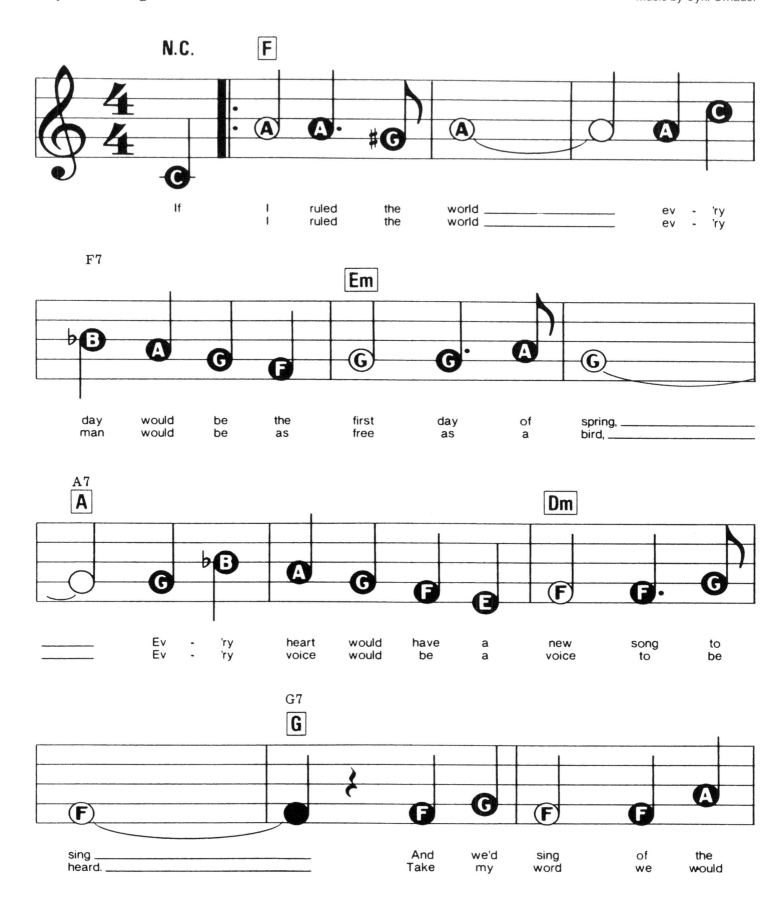

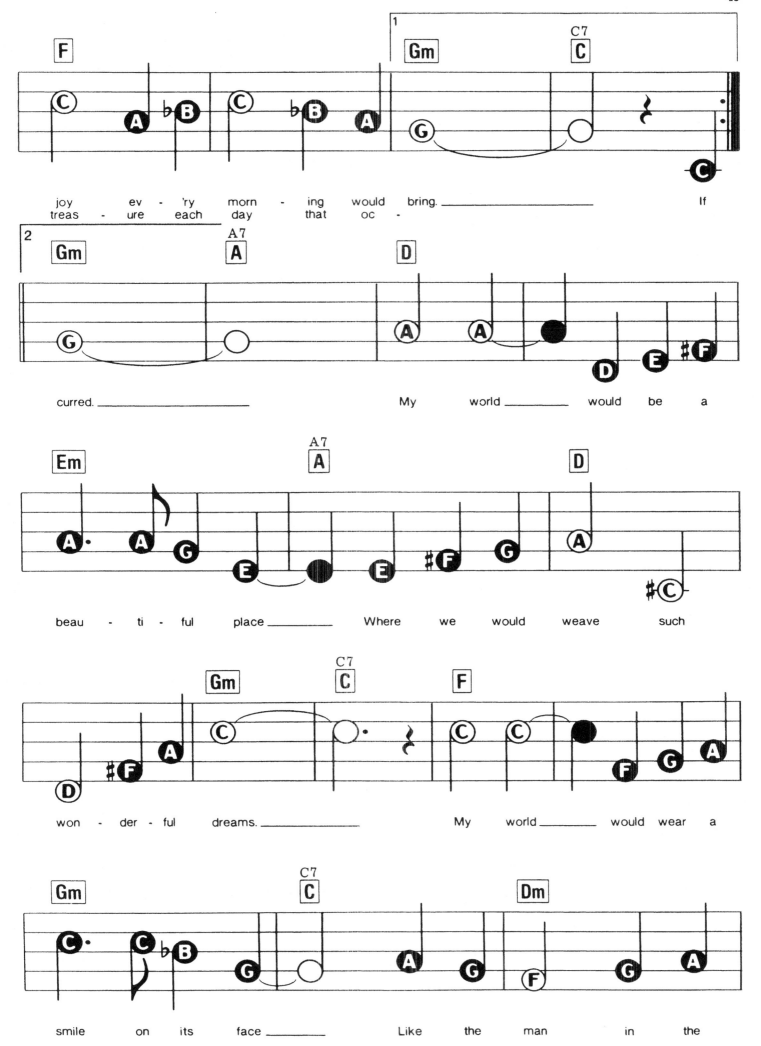

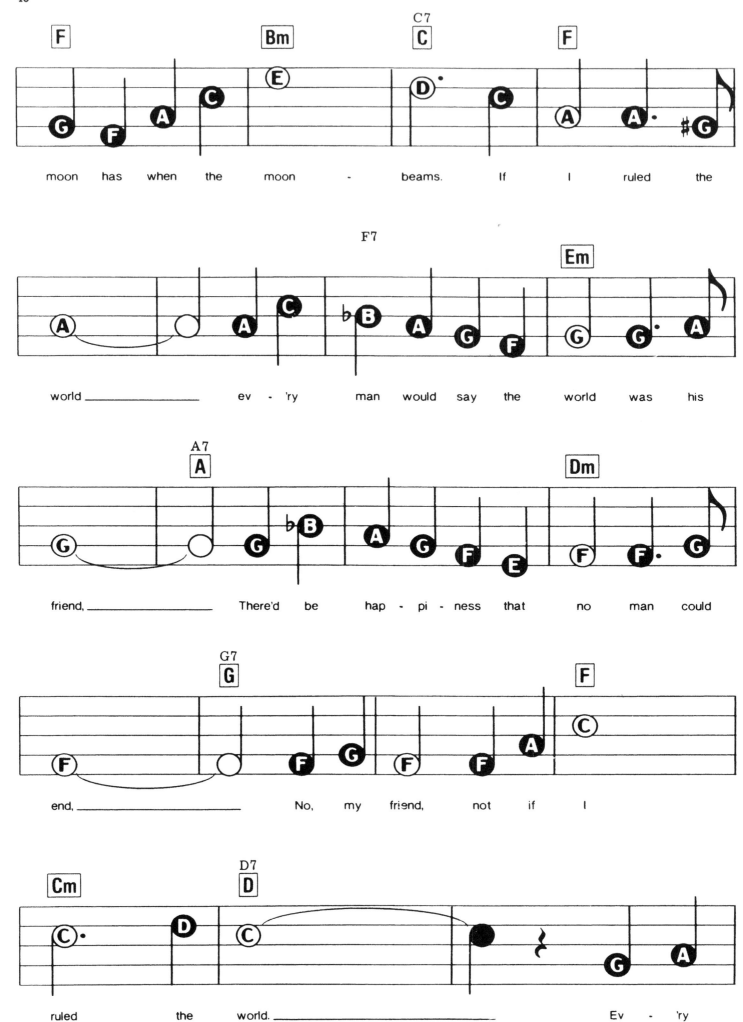

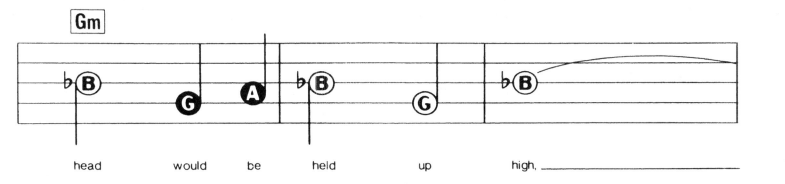

head would be held up high, _____

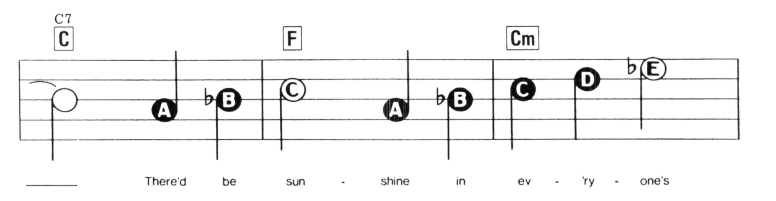

_____ There'd be sun - shine in ev - 'ry - one's

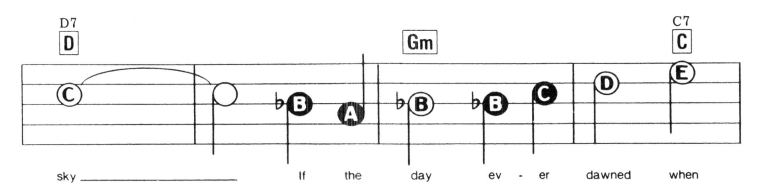

sky _____ If the day ev - er dawned when

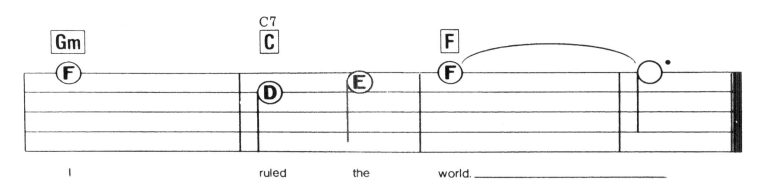

I ruled the world. _____

If We Only Have Love
(Quand On N'a Que L'amour)
from JACQUES BREL IS ALIVE AND WELL AND LIVING IN PARIS

Registration 4
Rhythm: Ballad

French Words and Music by Jacques Brel
English Words by Mort Shuman and Eric Blau

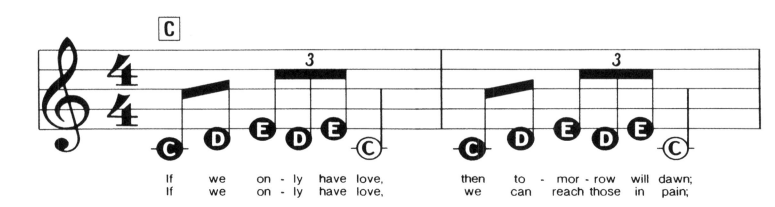

If we on-ly have love,   then to-mor-row will dawn;
If we on-ly have love,   we can reach those in pain;

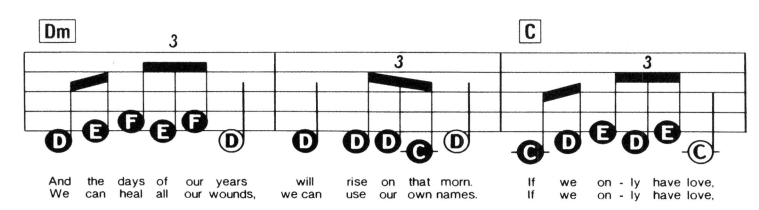

And the days of our years   will rise on that morn.   If we on-ly have love,
We can heal all our wounds,   we can use our own names.   If we on-ly have love,

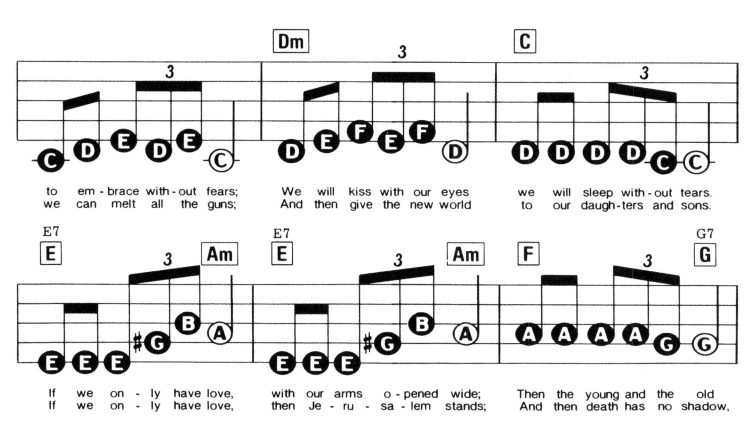

to em-brace with-out fears;   We will kiss with our eyes   we will sleep with-out tears.
we can melt all the guns;   And then give the new world   to our daugh-ters and sons.

If we on-ly have love,   with our arms o-pened wide;   Then the young and the old
If we on-ly have love,   then Je-ru-sa-lem stands;   And then death has no shadow,

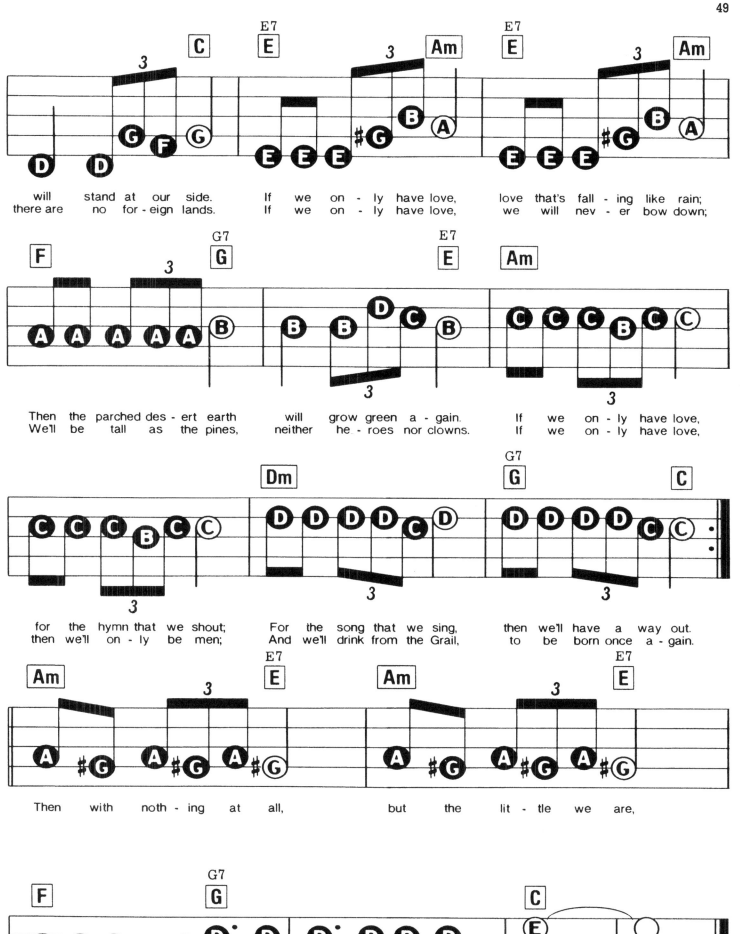

will   stand   at   our   side.   If   we   on - ly   have love,   love that's fall - ing like rain;
there are   no   for-eign lands.   If   we   on - ly   have love,   we   will   nev - er bow down;

Then   the   parched des - ert earth   will   grow green a - gain.   If   we   on - ly   have love,
We'll   be   tall   as   the pines,   neither he - roes nor clowns.   If   we   on - ly   have love,

for   the   hymn that we shout;   For   the   song that we sing,   then we'll have   a   way out.
then we'll on - ly   be   men;   And   we'll drink from the Grail,   to   be   born once a - gain.

Then   with noth - ing   at   all,   but   the   lit - tle we   are,

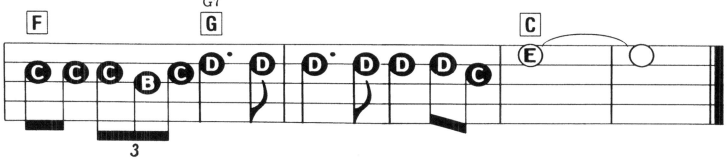

We'll have con-quered all time,   all   space,   the sun, and the   stars._____

Give Peace a Chance

Registration 5
Rhythm: Rock or Jazz Rock

Words and Music by
John Lennon

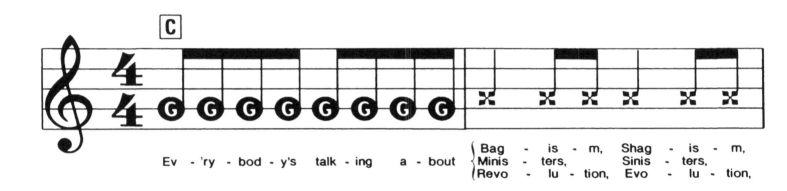

Ev - 'ry - bod - y's talk - ing a - bout
{ Bag - is - m, Shag - is - m,
Minis - ters, Sinis - ters,
Revo - lu - tion, Evo - lu - tion,

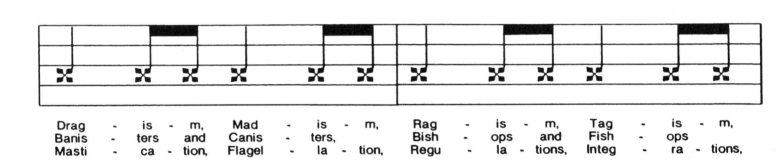

Drag - is - m, Mad - is - m, Rag - is - m, Tag - is - m,
Banis - ters and Canis - ters, Bish - ops and Fish - ops
Masti - ca - tion, Flagel - la - tion, Regu - la - tions, Integ - ra - tions,

This - is - m, That - is - m, Is - n't it the most? }
Rab - bis and Pop - eyes, Bye bye bye byes. }
Medi - ta - tions, United Na - tions, Con - grat - u - lations. }

G7
G

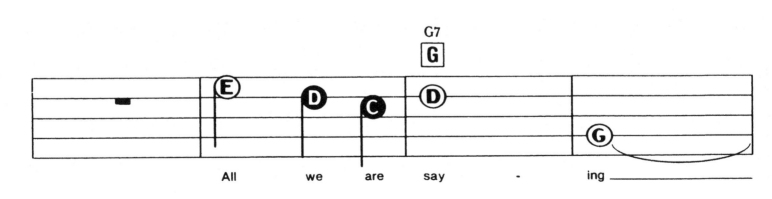

All we are say - ing _____

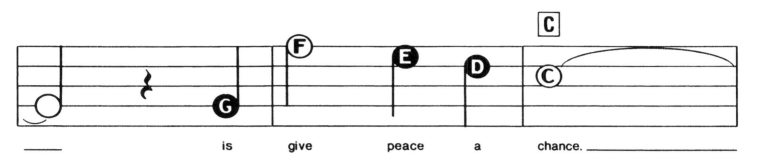

is give peace a chance. _____

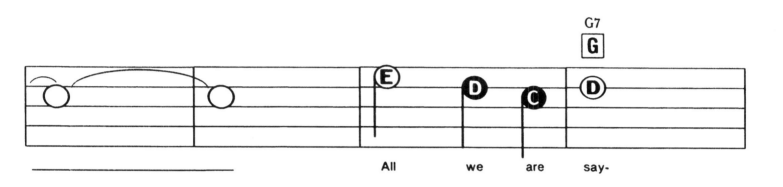

_____ All we are say-

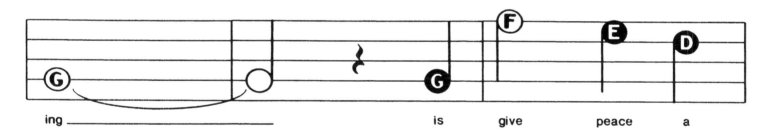

ing _____ is give peace a

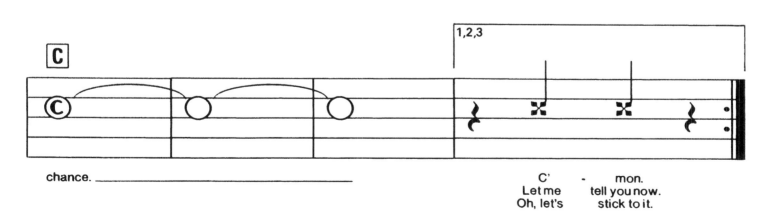

chance. _____   C' - mon.
                          Let me   tell you now.
                          Oh, let's   stick to it.

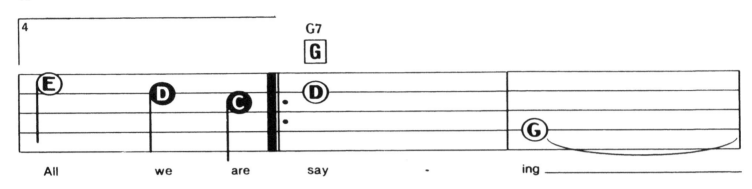

All   we   are   say - ing

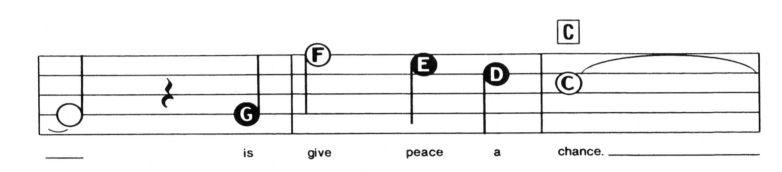

is   give   peace   a   chance.

Repeat and Fade

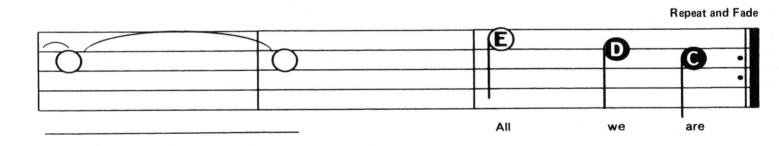

All   we   are

4. Ev'rybody's talking about
John and Yoko, Timmy Leary, Rosemary, Tommy Smothers,
Bobby Dylan, Tommy Cooper, Derek Taylor, Norman Mailer,
Alan Ginsberg, Hare Krishna, Hare, Hare Krishna
(Repeat Refrain)

Imagine

Registration 8
Rhythm: Rock or Slow Rock

Words and Music by
John Lennon

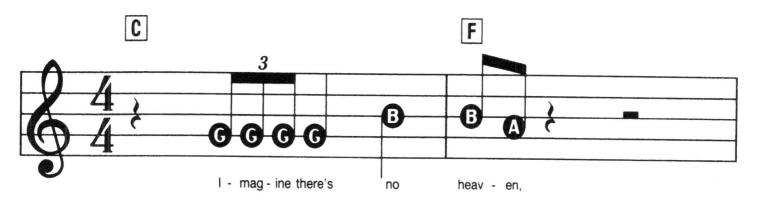

I - mag - ine there's no heav - en,

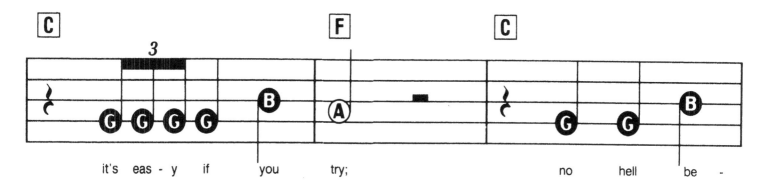

it's eas - y if you try; no hell be -

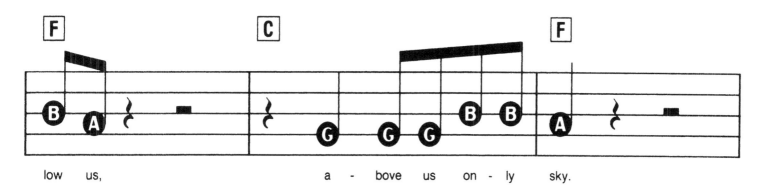

low us, a - bove us on - ly sky.

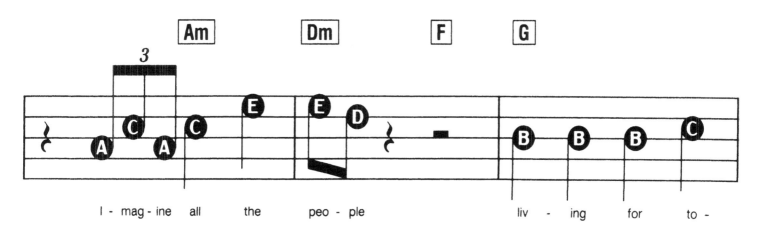

I - mag - ine all the peo - ple liv - ing for to -

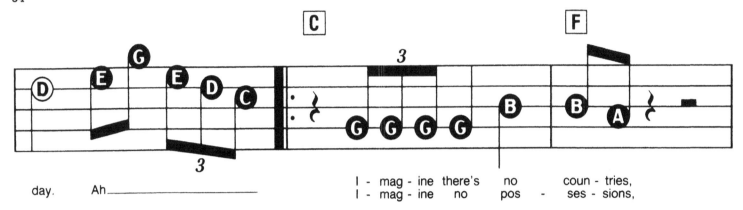

day. Ah_____

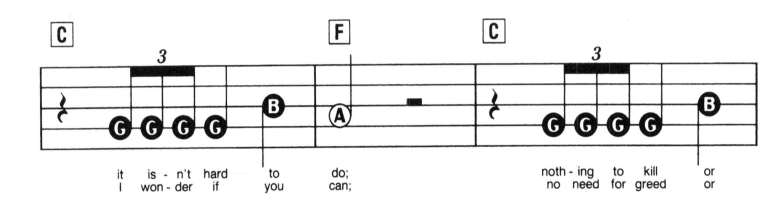

I - mag - ine there's   no   coun - tries,
I - mag - ine   no   pos -   ses - sions,

it   is - n't hard   to   do;
I   won - der   if   you   can;

noth - ing   to   kill   or
no   need for greed   or

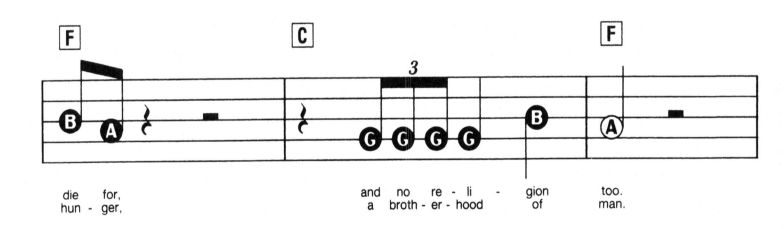

die   for,
hun - ger,

and no   re - li - gion   too.
a broth - er - hood of   man.

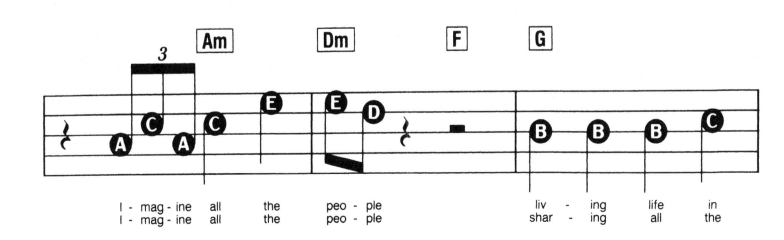

I - mag - ine   all   the   peo - ple
I - mag - ine   all   the   peo - ple

liv - ing   life   in
shar - ing   all   the

55

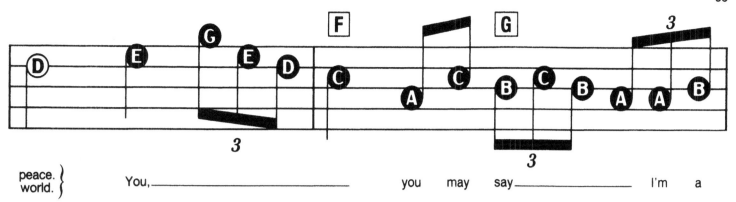

peace.
world. }

You,_____ you may say_____ I'm a

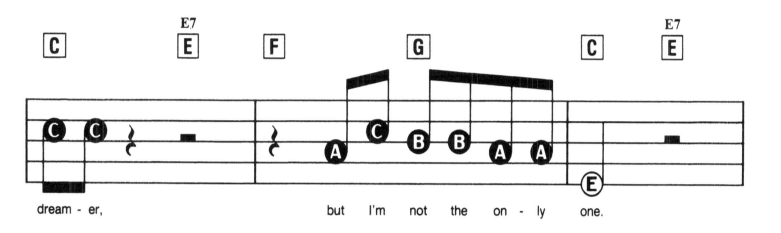

dream - er,   but I'm not the on - ly one.

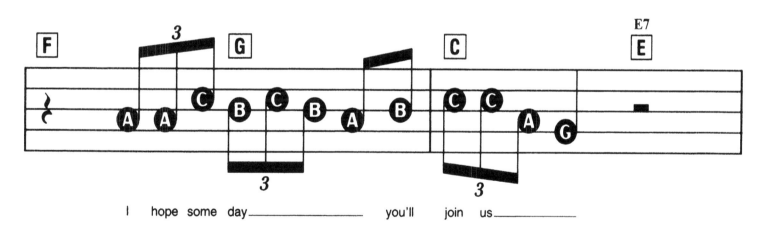

I   hope some day_____ you'll   join us_____

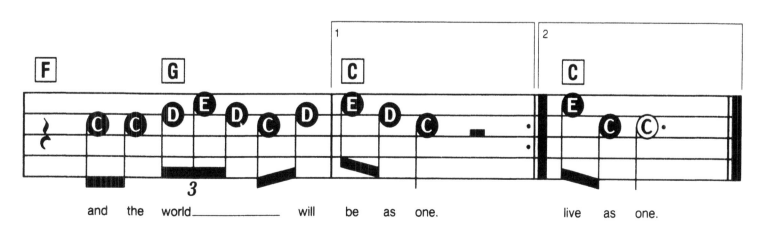

and   the world_____ will   be   as   one.   live as one.

The Impossible Dream
(The Quest)
from MAN OF LA MANCHA

Registration 3
Rhythm: Waltz

Lyric by Joe Darion
Music by Mitch Leigh

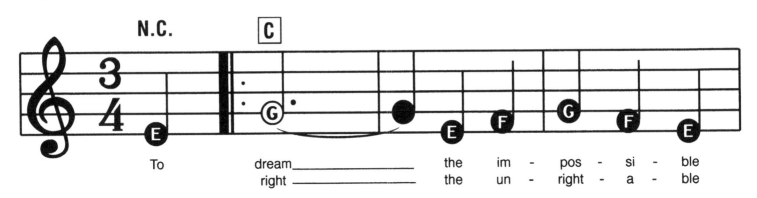

To
dream _____ the im - pos - si - ble
right _____ the un - right - a - ble

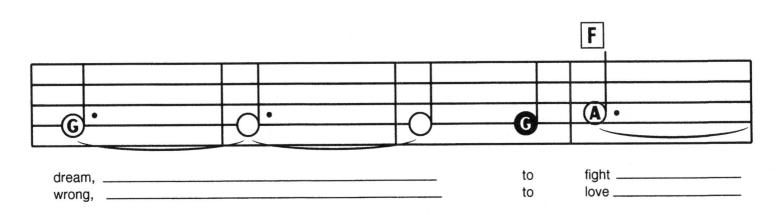

dream, _____ to fight _____
wrong, _____ to love _____

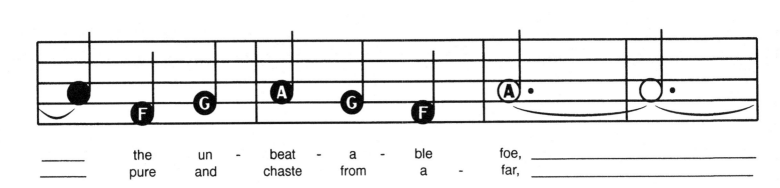

_____ the un - beat - a - ble foe, _____
_____ pure and chaste from a - far, _____

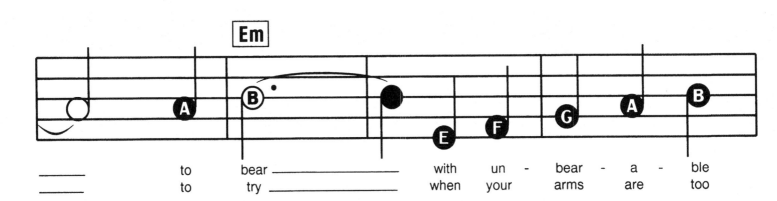

_____ to bear _____ with un - bear - a - ble
_____ to try _____ when your arms are too

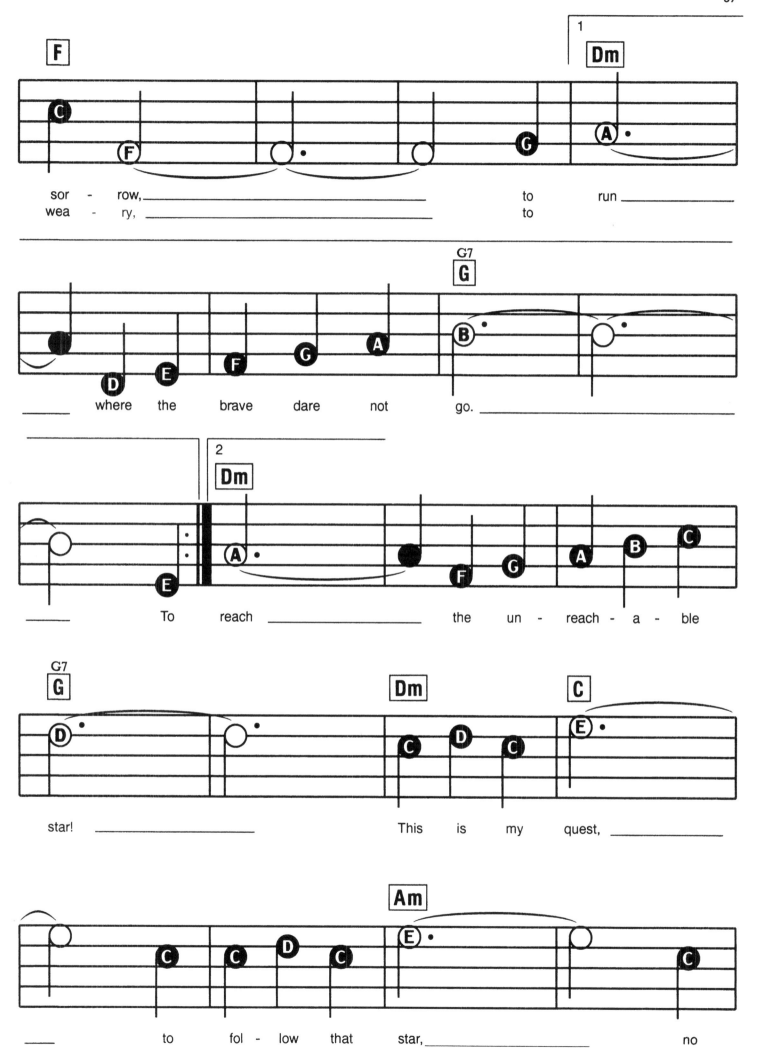

sor - row,_____ to run _____
wea - ry,_____ to

_____ where the brave dare not go. _____

_____ To reach _____ the un - reach - a - ble

star! _____ This is my quest, _____

_____ to fol - low that star,_____ no

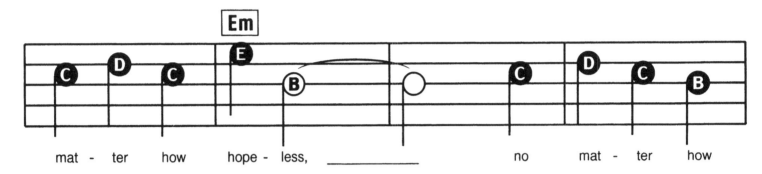

mat - ter how hope - less, _____ no mat - ter how

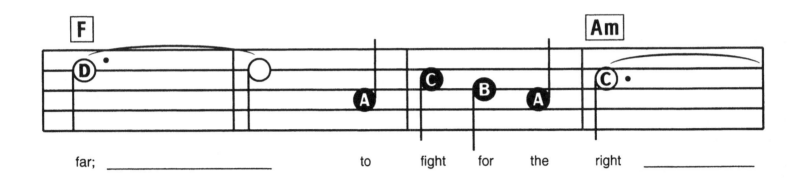

far; _____ to fight for the right _____

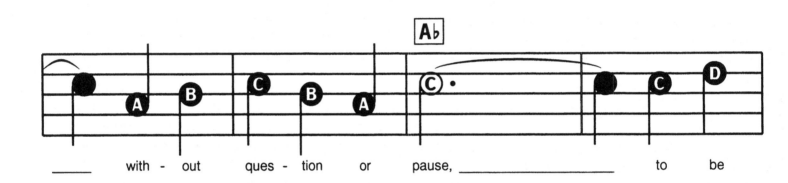

_____ with - out ques - tion or pause, _____ to be

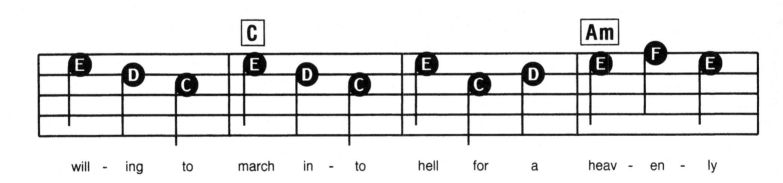

will - ing to march in - to hell for a heav - en - ly

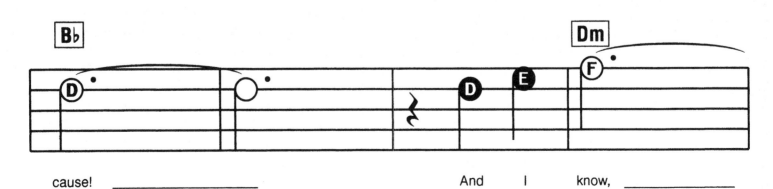

cause! _____ And I know, _____

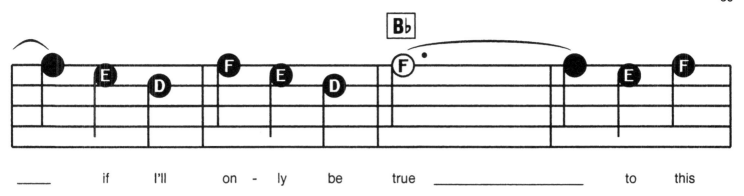

if I'll on - ly be true _____ to this

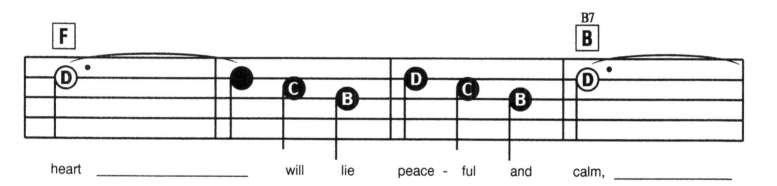

glo - ri - ous quest _____ that my

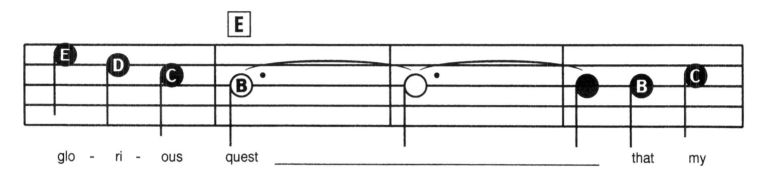

heart _____ will lie peace - ful and calm, _____

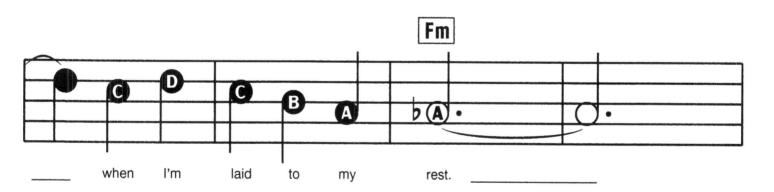

when I'm laid to my rest. _____

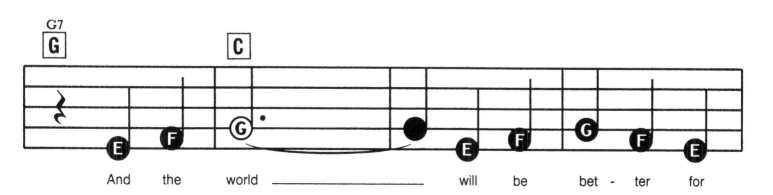

And the world _____ will be bet - ter for

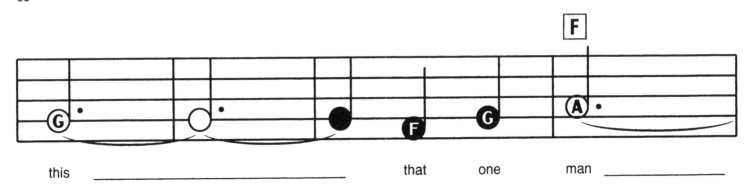

this _____ that one man _____

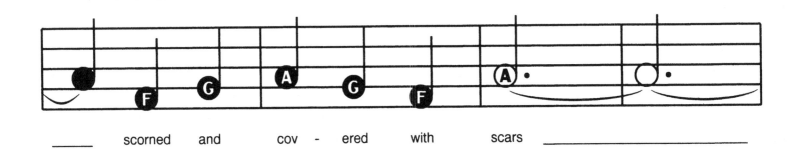

_____ scorned and cov - ered with scars _____

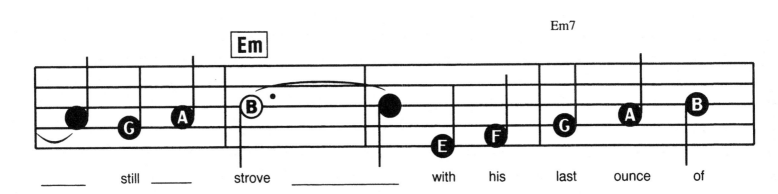

_____ still _____ strove _____ with his last ounce of

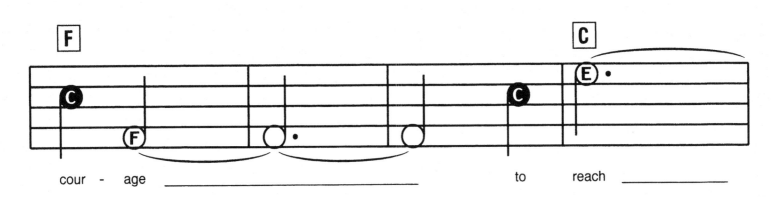

cour - age _____ to reach _____

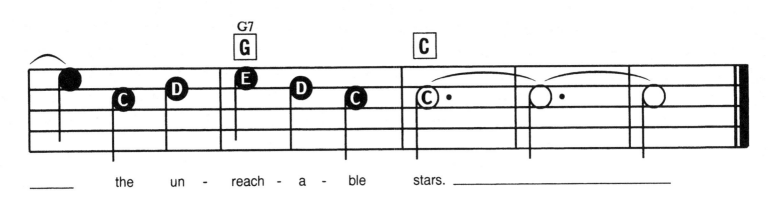

_____ the un - reach - a - ble stars. _____

Lost in the Stars
from the Musical Production LOST IN THE STARS

Registration 9
Rhythm: Ballad

Words by Maxwell Anderson
Music by Kurt Weill

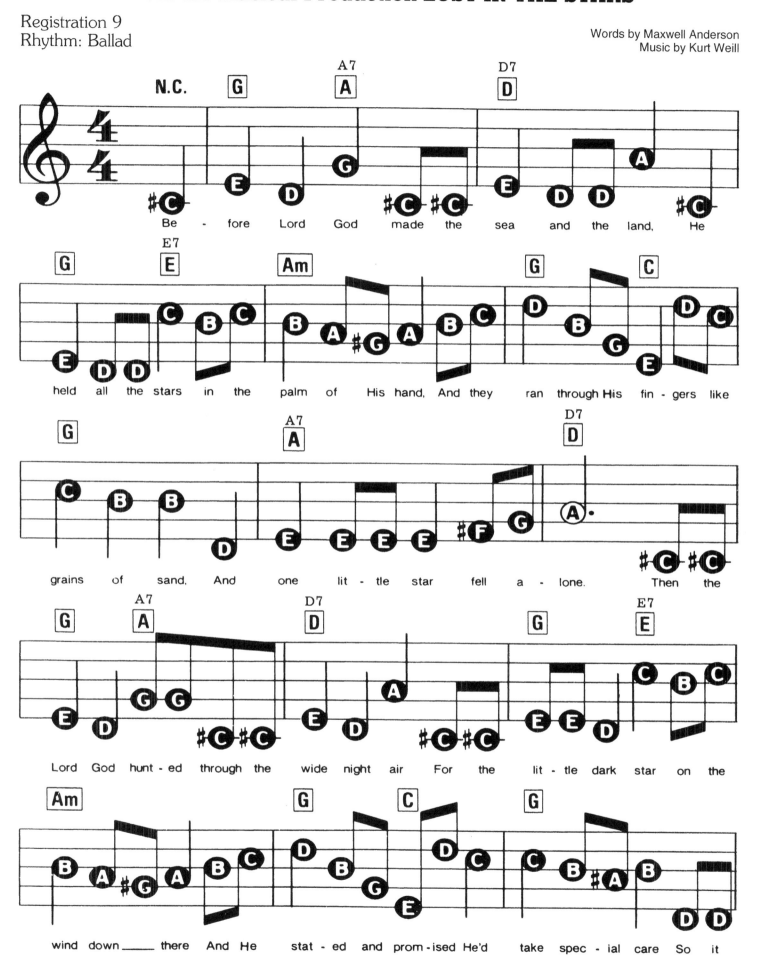

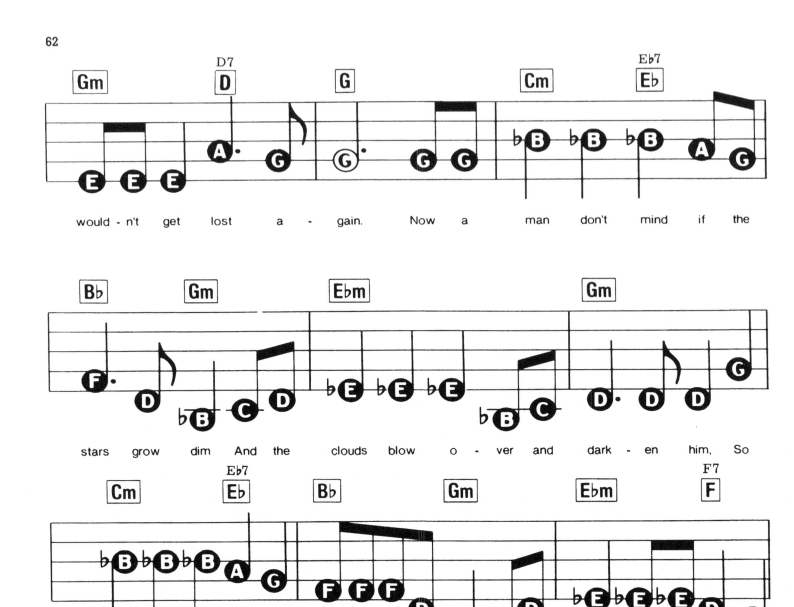

would-n't get lost a - gain. Now a man don't mind if the

stars grow dim And the clouds blow o - ver and dark - en him, So

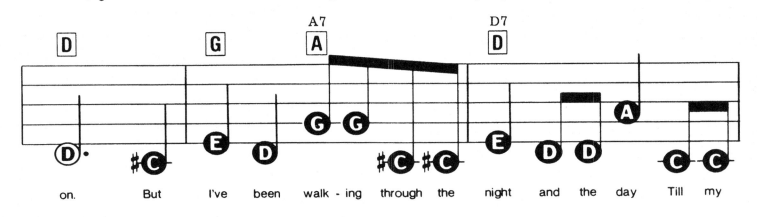

long as the Lord God's watch-ing o - ver them, Keep-ing track how it all goes

on. But I've been walk-ing through the night and the day Till my

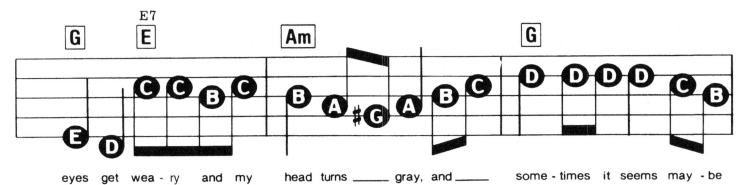

eyes get wea - ry and my head turns _____ gray, and _____ some - times it seems may - be

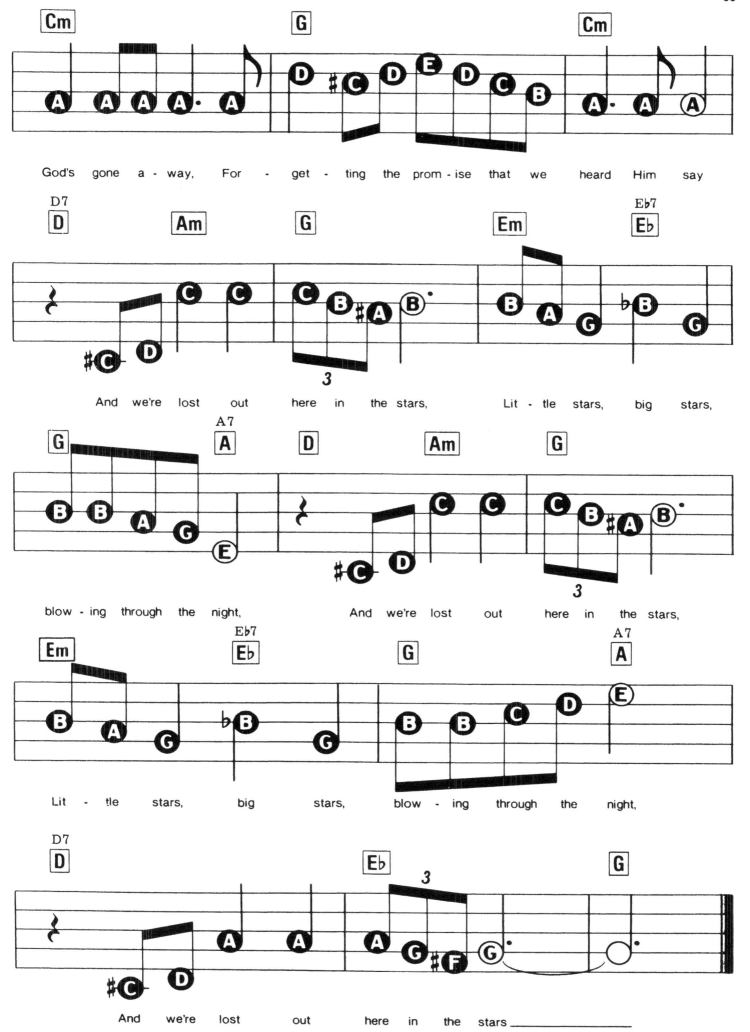

The Rainbow Connection
from THE MUPPET MOVIE

Registration 4
Rhythm: Waltz

Words and Music by Paul Williams
and Kenneth L. Ascher

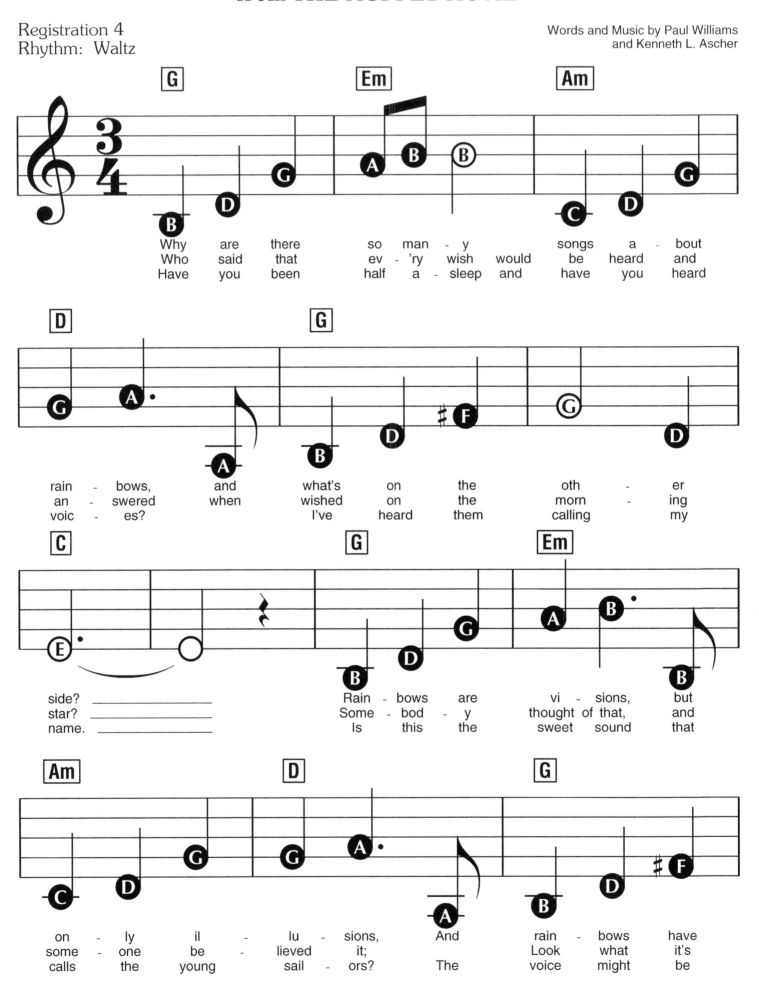

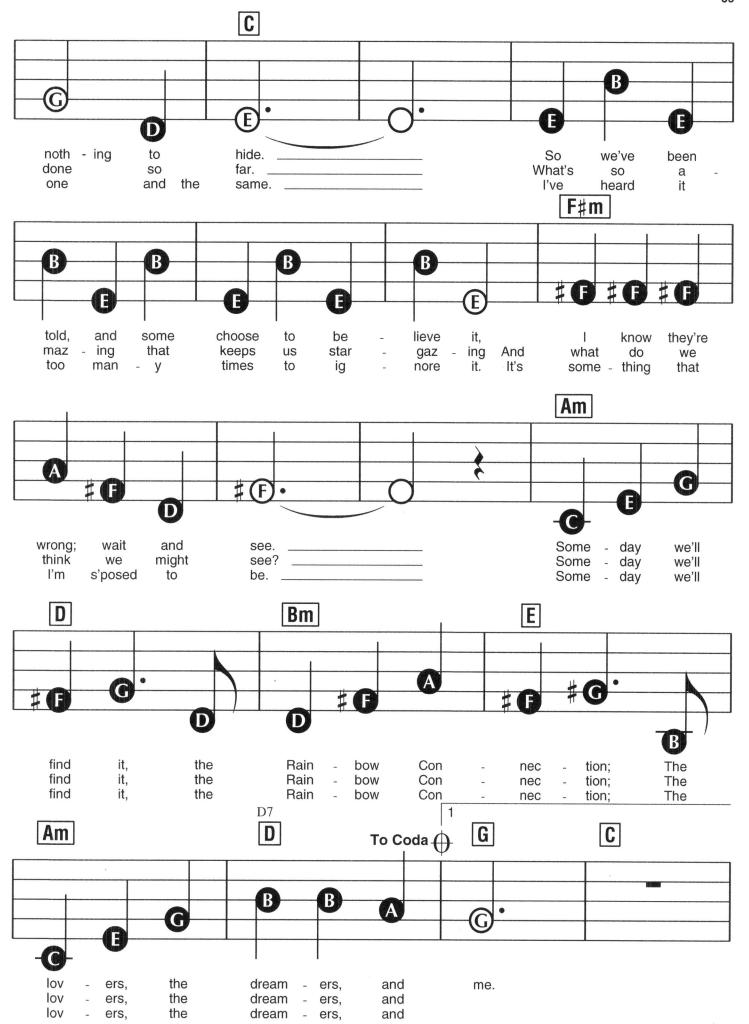

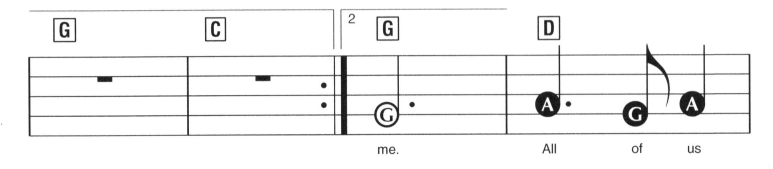

me.   All   of   us

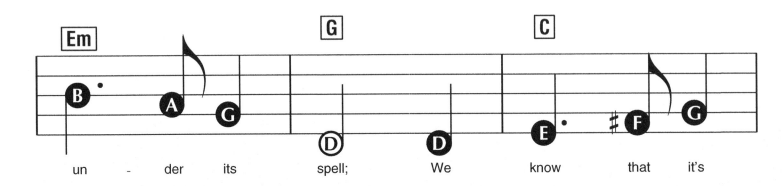

un - der   its   spell;   We   know   that   it's

D.C. al Coda
(Return to beginning
Play to ⊕ and
Skip to Coda)

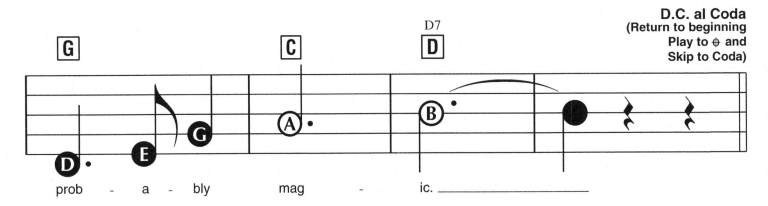

prob - a - bly   mag - ic. _____

CODA

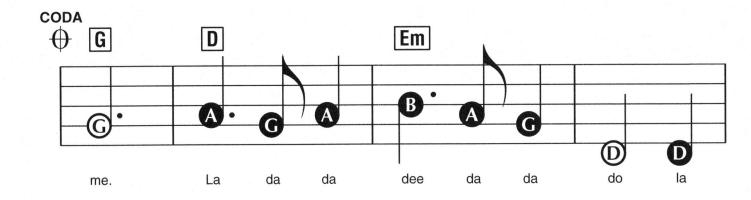

me.   La   da   da   dee   da   da   do   la

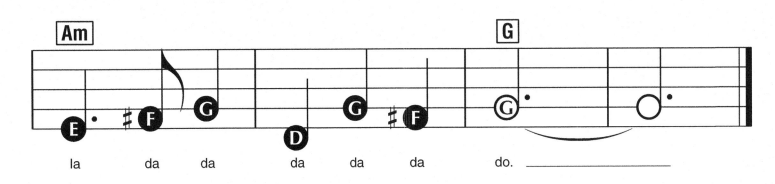

la   da   da   da   da   da   do. _____

Tears in Heaven

Registration 8
Rhythm: 8 Beat

Words and Music by Eric Clapton
and Will Jennings

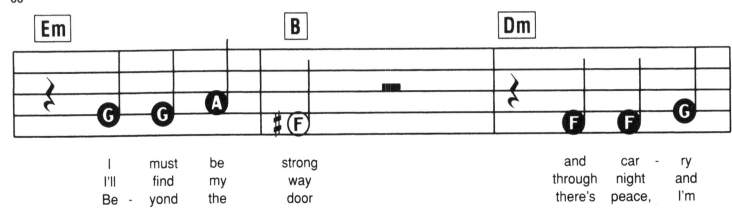

I	must	be	strong
I'll	find	my	way
Be -	yond	the	door

and	car -	ry
through	night	and
there's	peace,	I'm

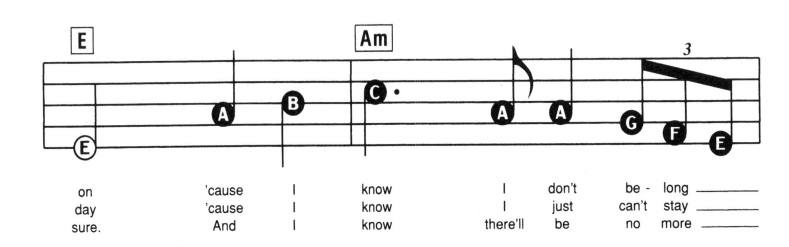

on	'cause	I	know
day	'cause	I	know
sure.	And	I	know

I	don't	be - long
I	just	can't stay
there'll	be	no more

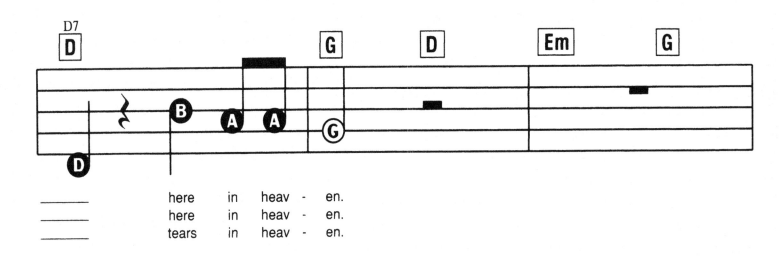

here	in	heav - en.
here	in	heav - en.
tears	in	heav - en.

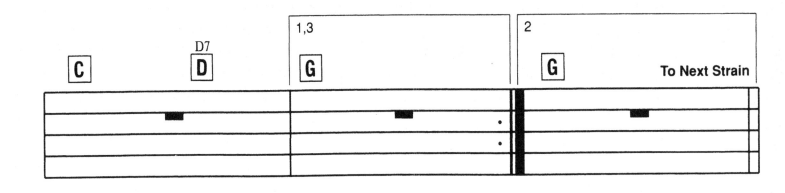

To Next Strain

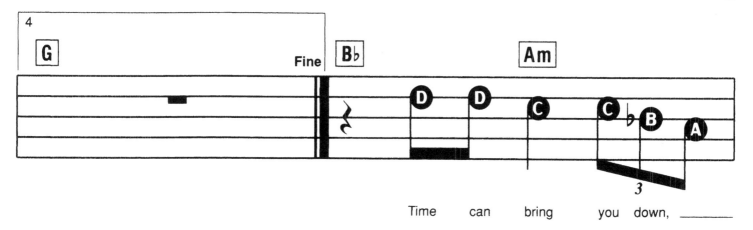

Time can bring you down, _____

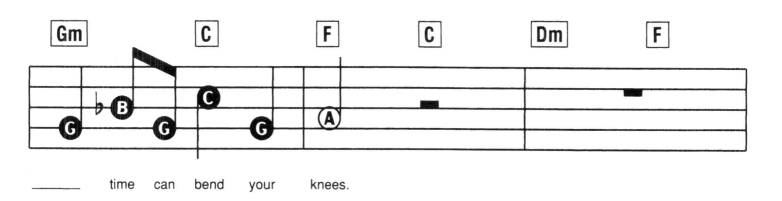

_____ time can bend your knees.

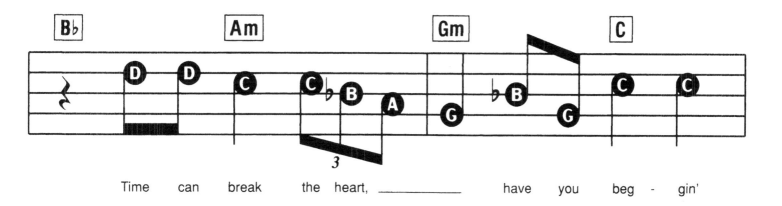

Time can break the heart, _____ have you beg - gin'

D.C. and Fade
(Return to beginning and Fade)

D7

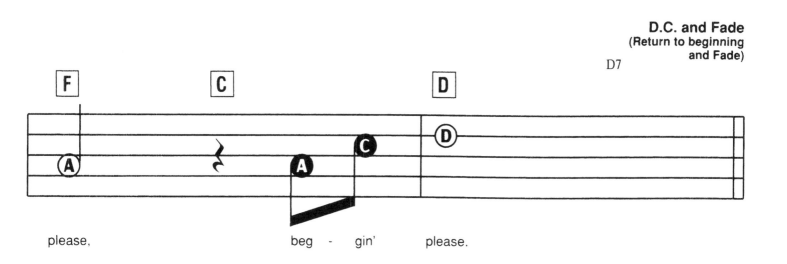

please, beg - gin' please.

Reach Out and Touch
(Somebody's Hand)

Registration 4
Rhythm: Waltz

Words and Music by Nickolas Ashford
and Valerie Simpson

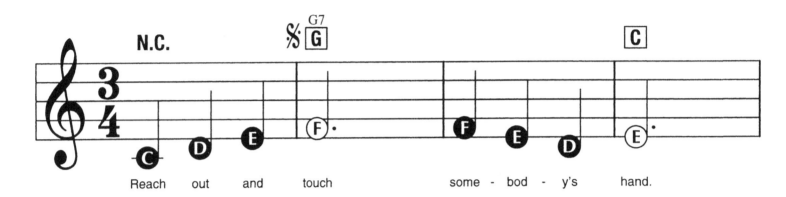

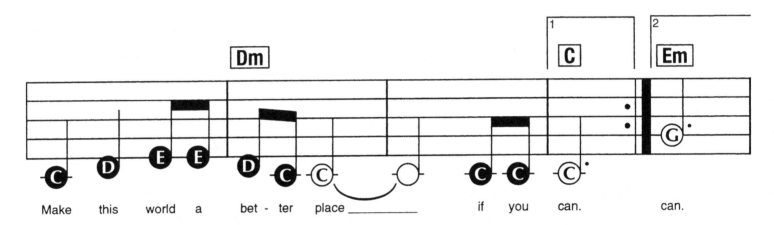

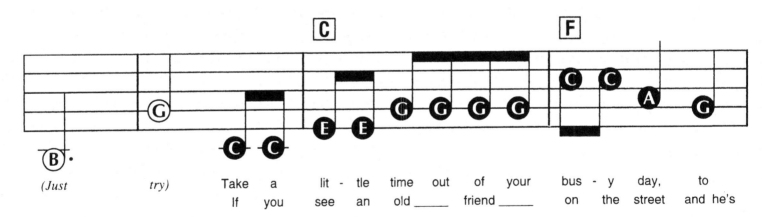

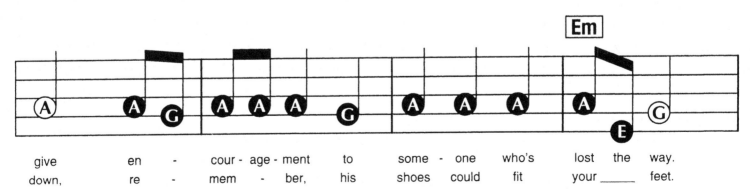

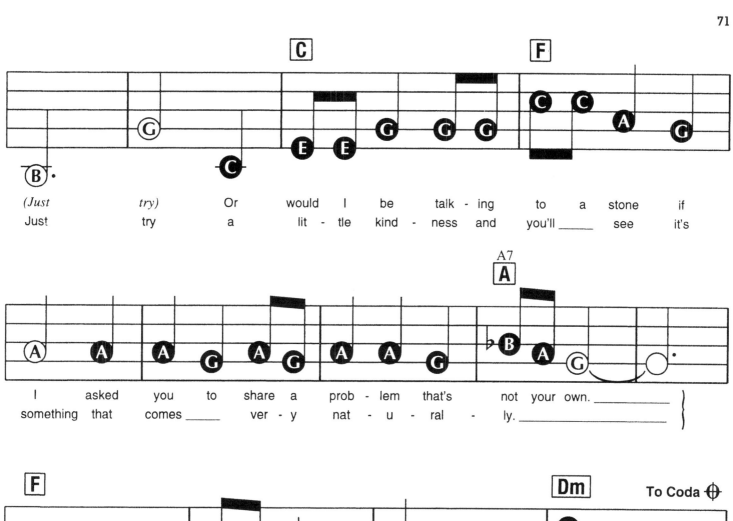

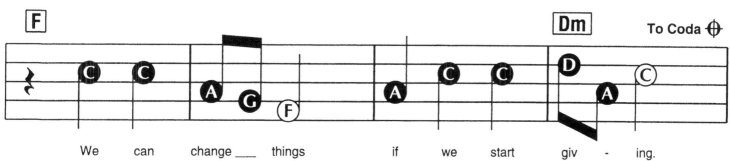

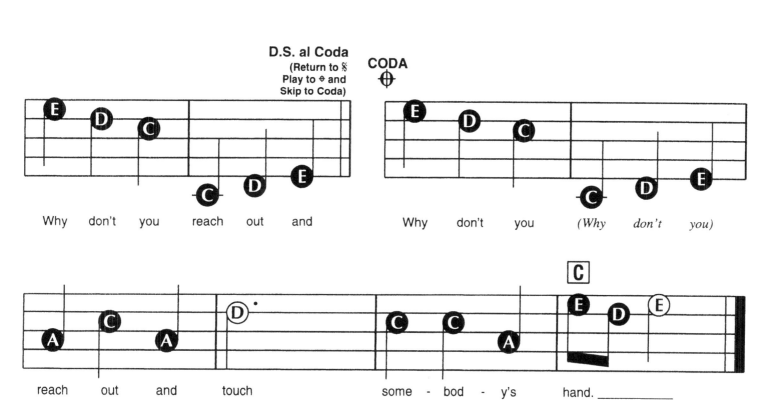

Tomorrow
from the Musical Production ANNIE

Registration 1
Rhythm: Swing or Jazz

Lyric by Martin Charnin
Music by Charles Strouse

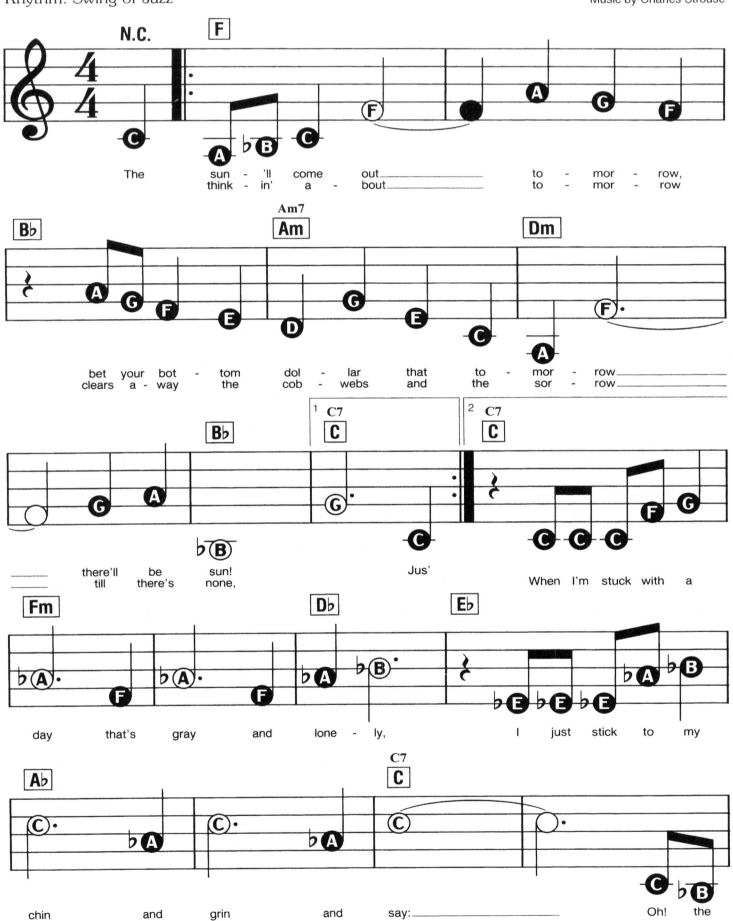

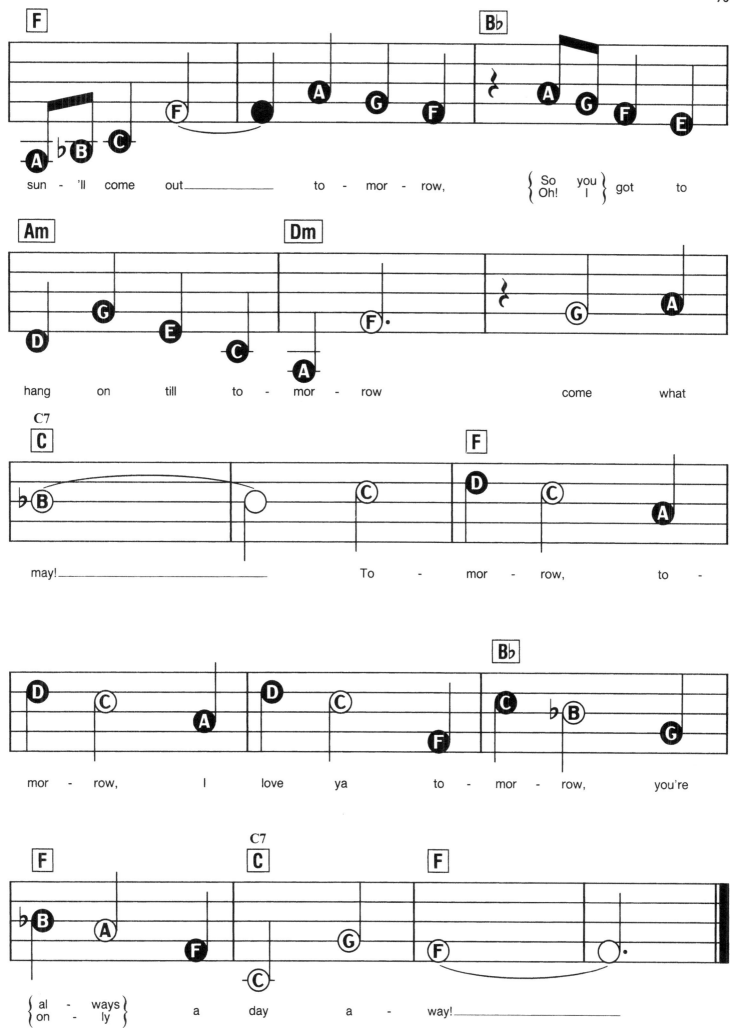

Turn! Turn! Turn!
(To Everything There Is a Season)

Registration 2
Rhythm: Ballad or Fox Trot

Words from the Book of Ecclesiastes
Adaptation and Music by Pete Seeger

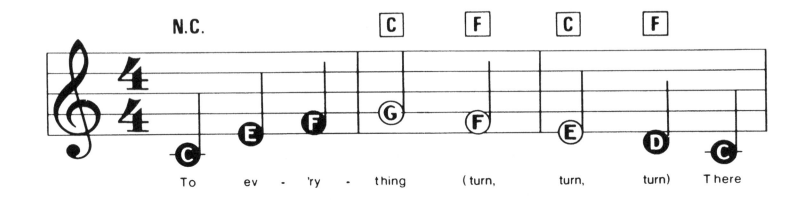

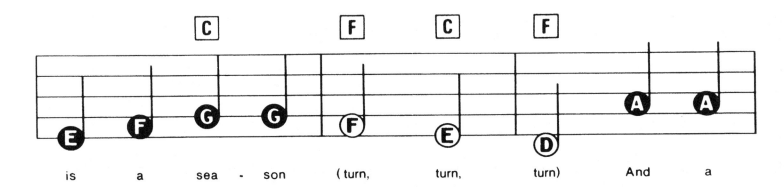

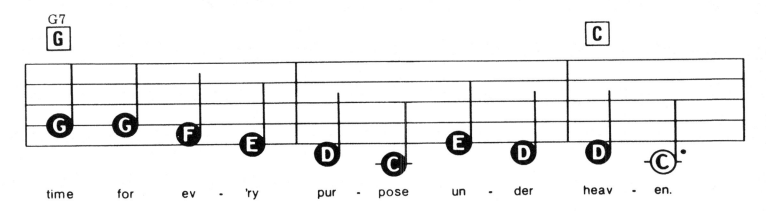

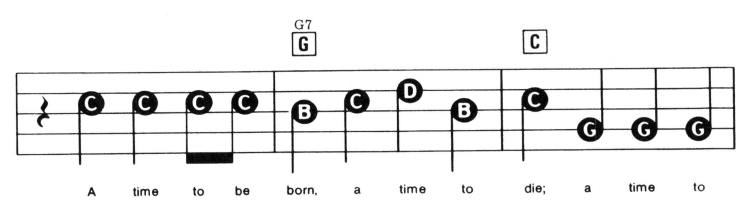

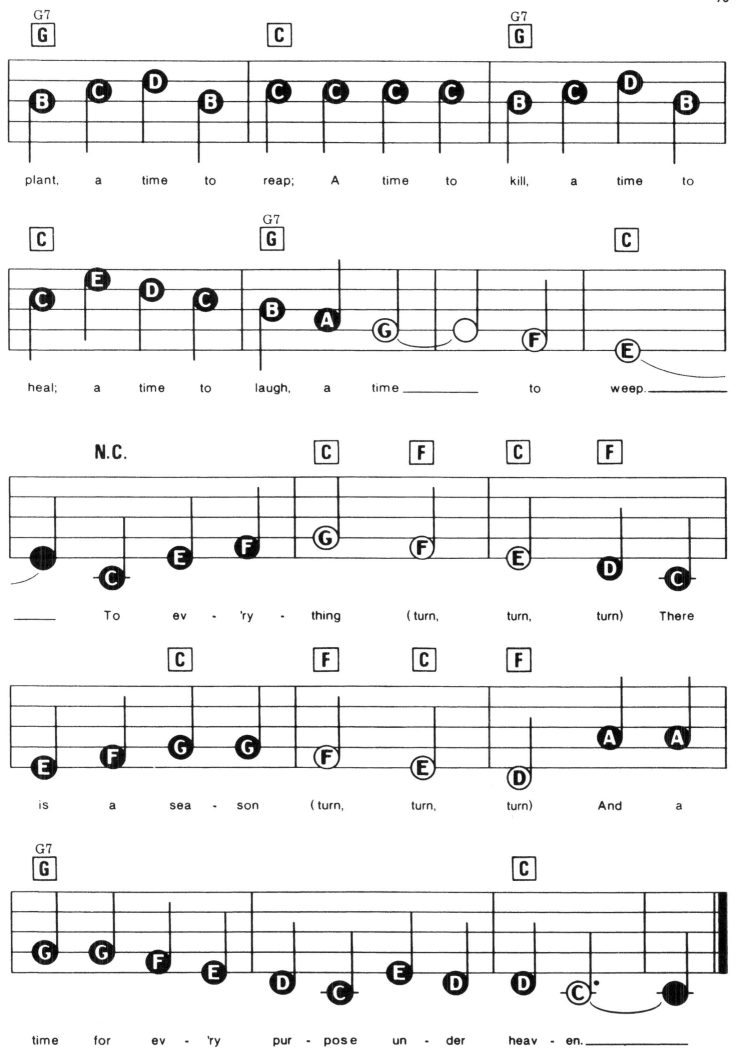

We Are the World

Registration 3
Rhythm: Pops or 8 Beat

Words and Music by Lionel Richie
and Michael Jackson

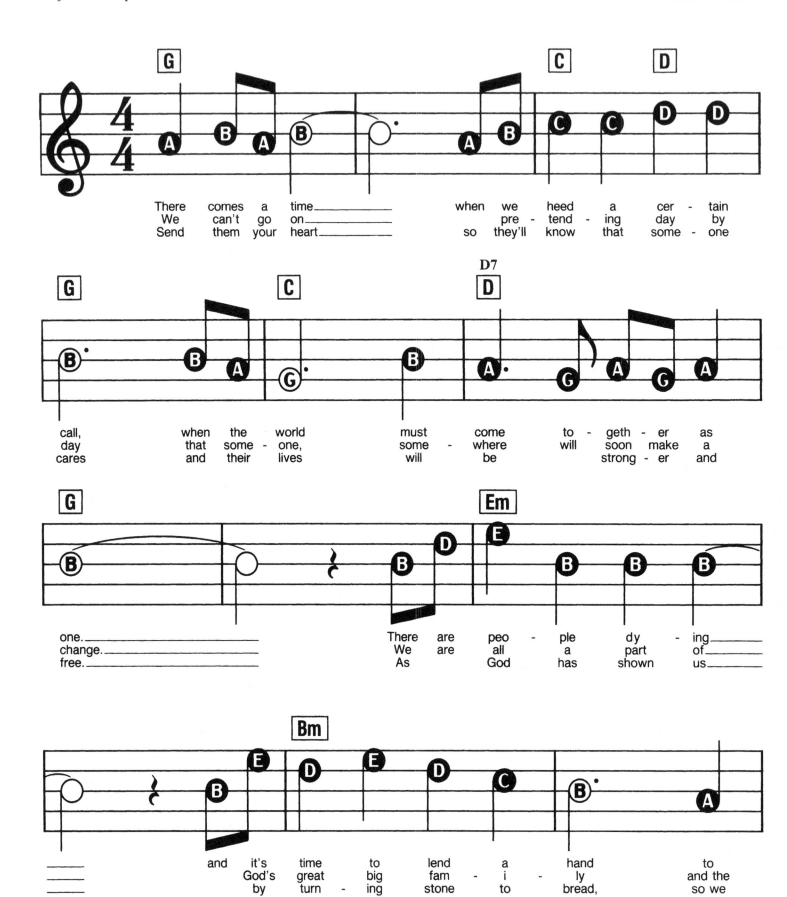

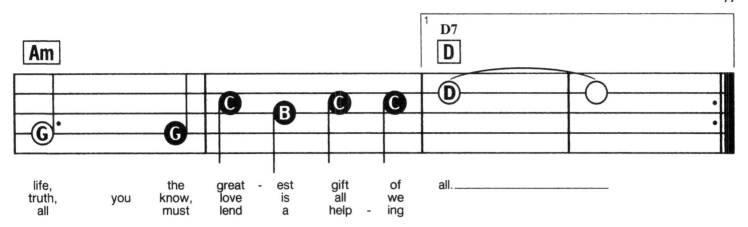

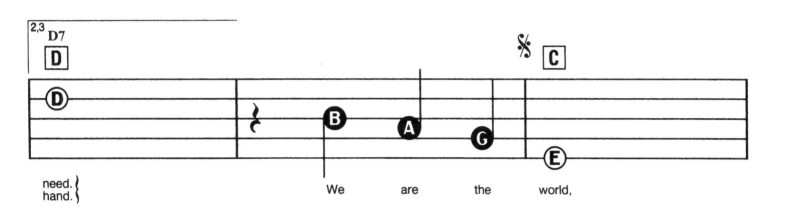

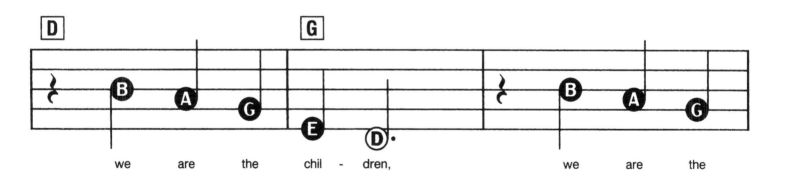

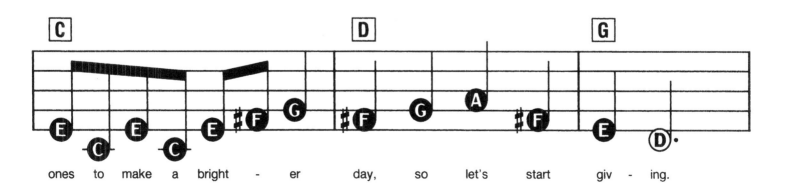

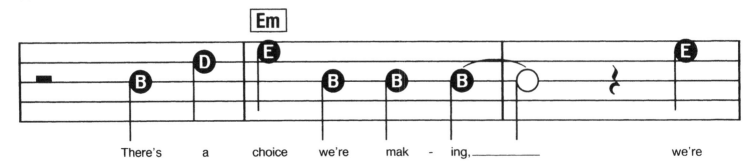

There's a choice we're mak - ing,_____ we're

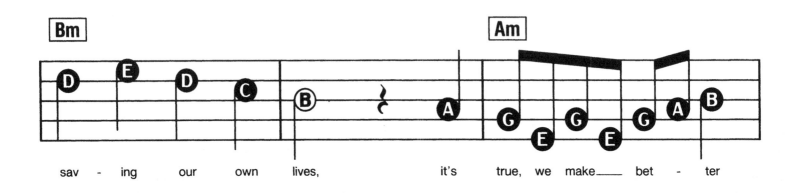

sav - ing our own lives, it's true, we make____ bet - ter

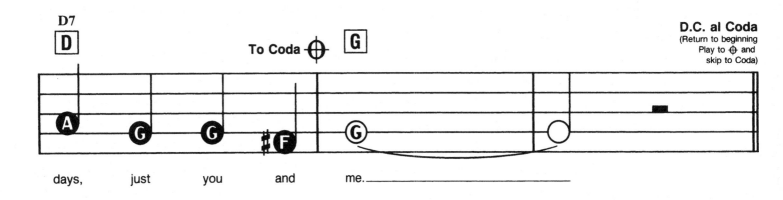

days, just you and me._____

D.C. al Coda
(Return to beginning
Play to ⊕ and
skip to Coda)

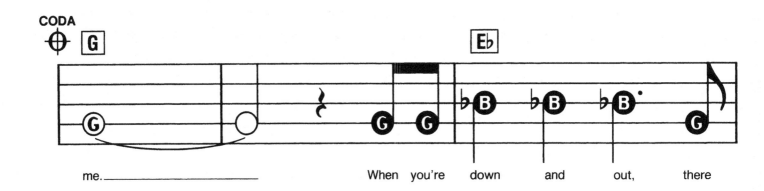

me._____ When you're down and out, there

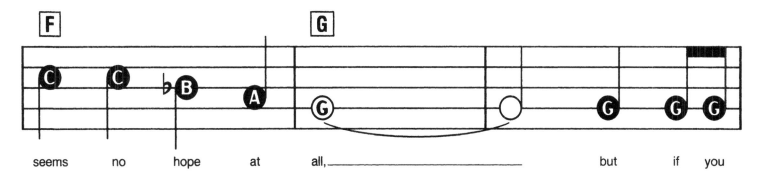

seems no hope at all,_____ but if you

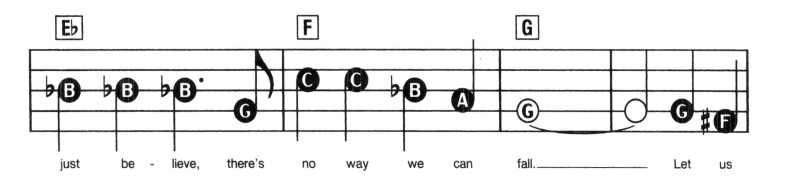

just be - lieve, there's no way we can fall._____ Let us

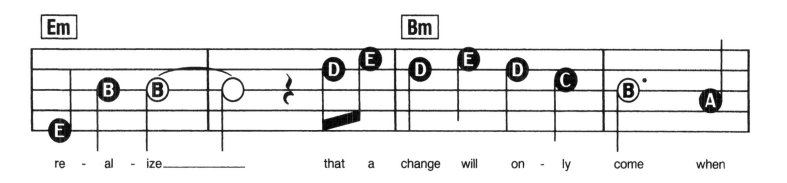

re - al - ize_____ that a change will on - ly come when

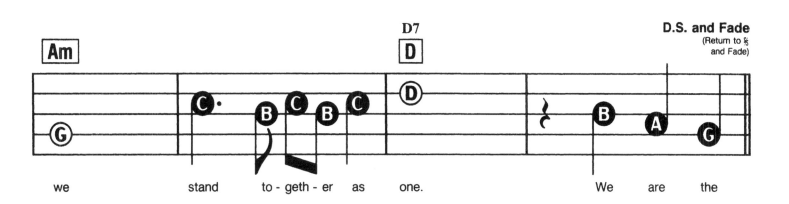

we stand to - geth - er as one. We are the

What a Wonderful World

Registration 2
Rhythm: Ballad

Words and Music by George David Weiss
and Bob Thiele

I see trees of green, red ros - es too, I see them bloom

for me and you. And I think to my - self, what a won - der - ful

world. _____ I see skies of blue and clouds of white, The

bright bles - sed day, the dark sac - red night. And I think to my - self,

What a won - der - ful world. _____ The col - ors of the rain - bow, so

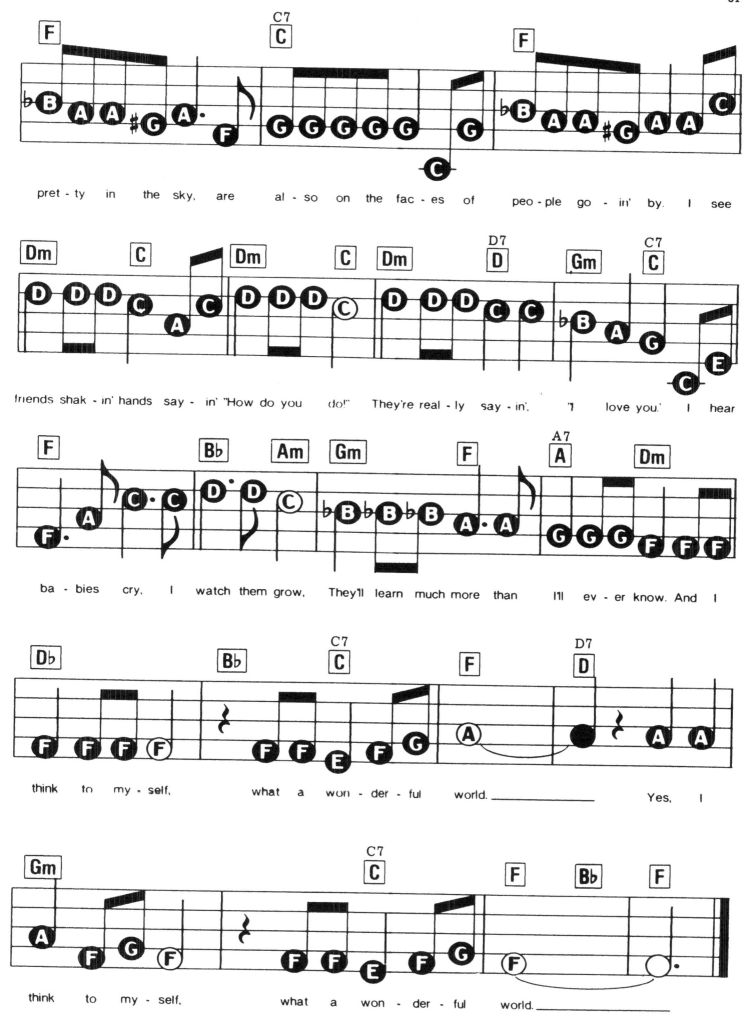

What the World Needs Now Is Love

Registration 2
Rhythm: Jazz Waltz or Waltz

Lyric by Hal David
Music by Burt Bacharach

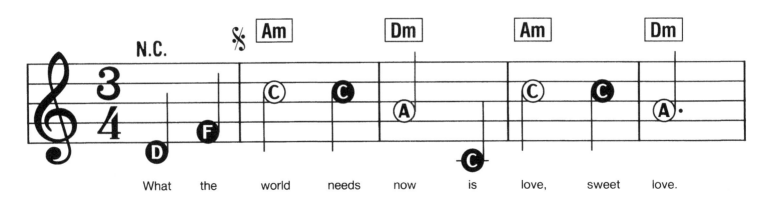

What the world needs now is love, sweet love.

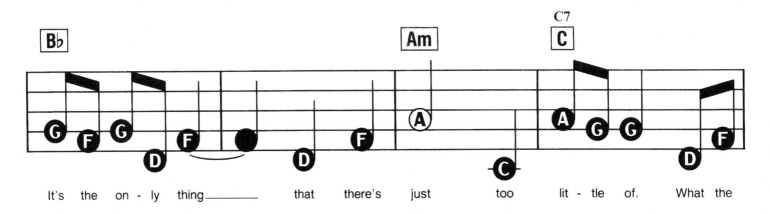

It's the on-ly thing_____ that there's just too lit-tle of. What the

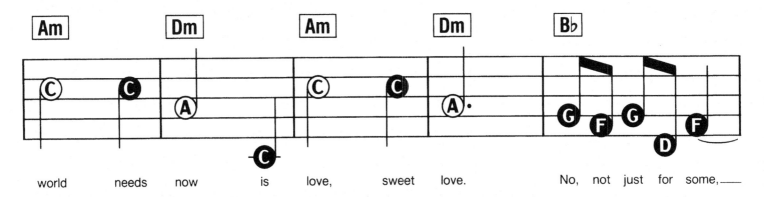

world needs now is love, sweet love. No, not just for some,_____

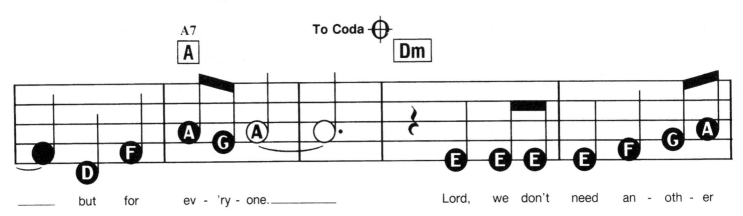

_____ but for ev-'ry-one._____ Lord, we don't need an-oth-er

83

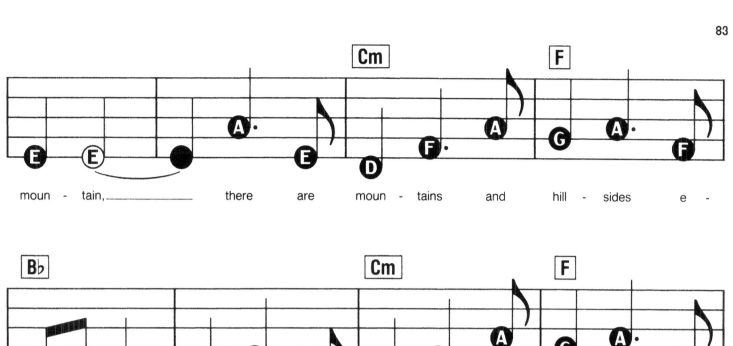

moun - tain,_____ there are moun - tains and hill - sides e -

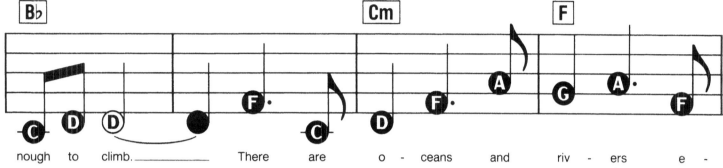

nough to climb._____ There are o - ceans and riv - ers e -

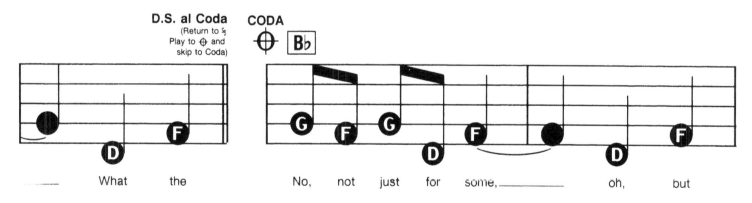

nough to cross, e - nough to last till the end of time._____

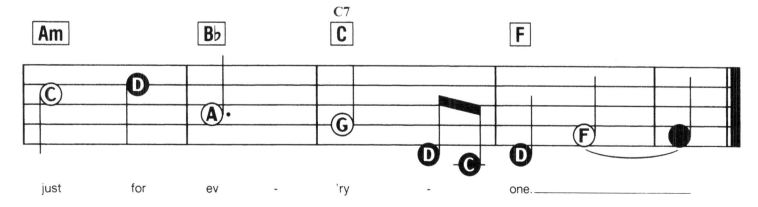

D.S. al Coda
(Return to 𝄋
Play to ⊕ and
skip to Coda)

CODA

What the   No, not just for some,_____ oh, but

just for ev - 'ry - one._____

With a Little Help from My Friends

Registration 5
Rhythm: Swing or Shuffle

Words and Music by John Lennon
and Paul McCartney

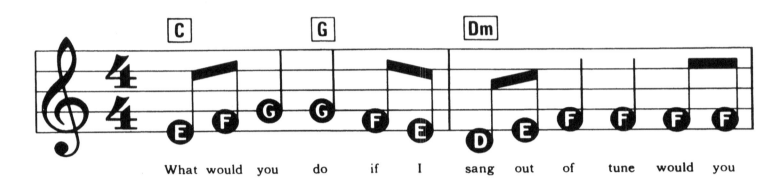

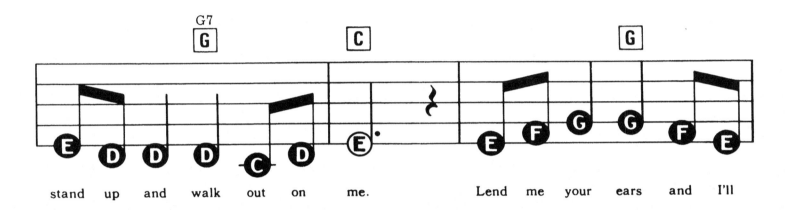

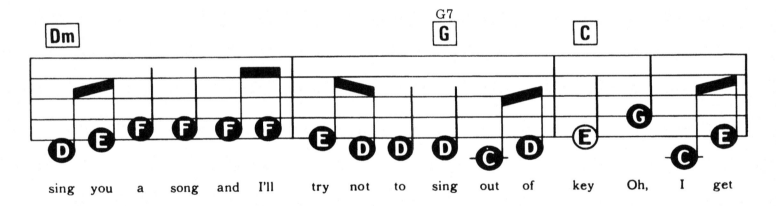

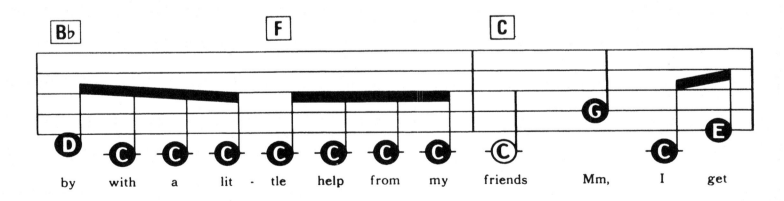

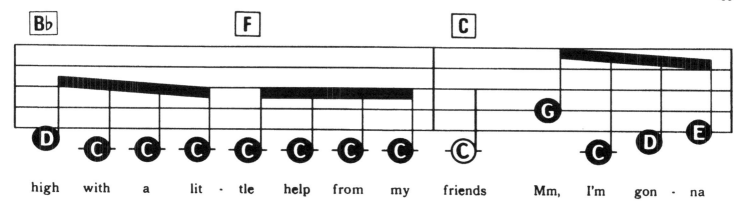

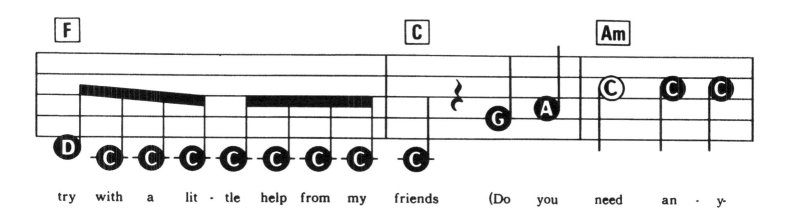

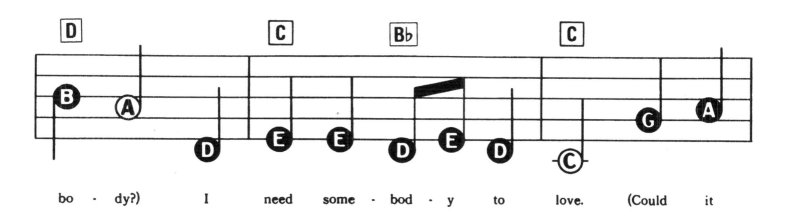

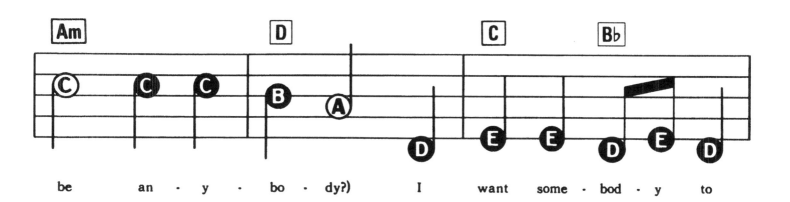

86

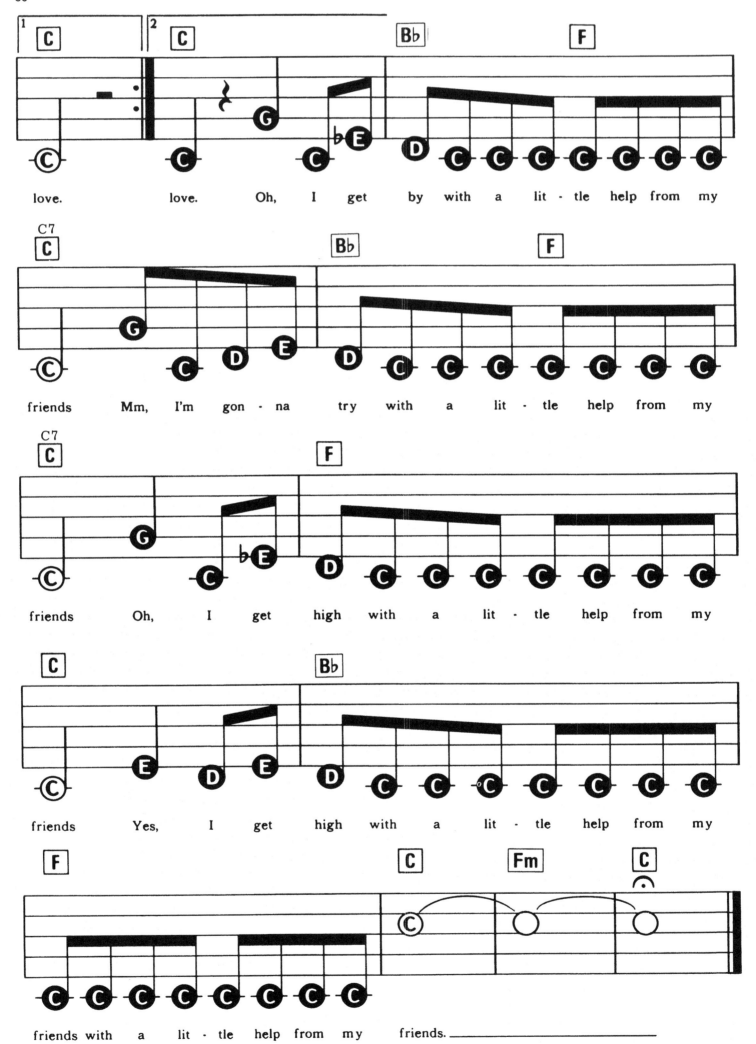

You Raise Me Up

Registration 3
Rhythm: Ballad

Words and Music by Brendan Graham
and Rolf Lovland

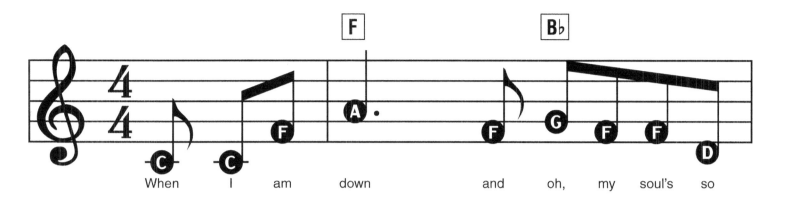

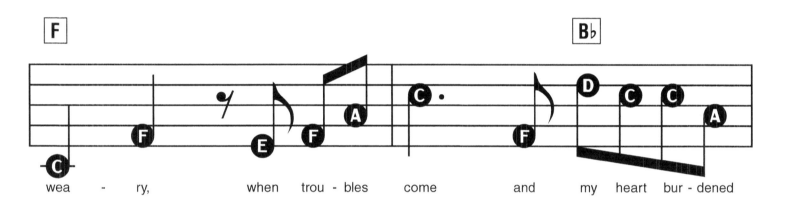

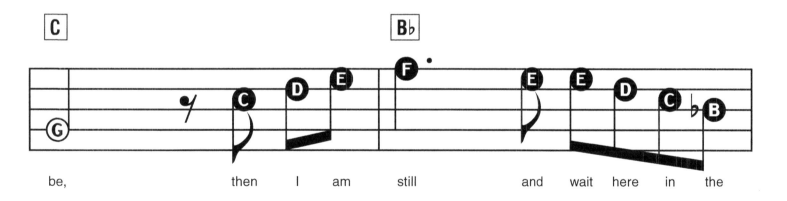

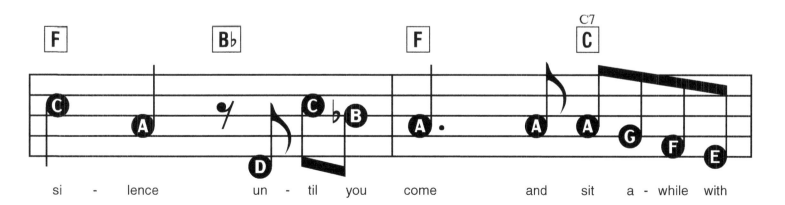

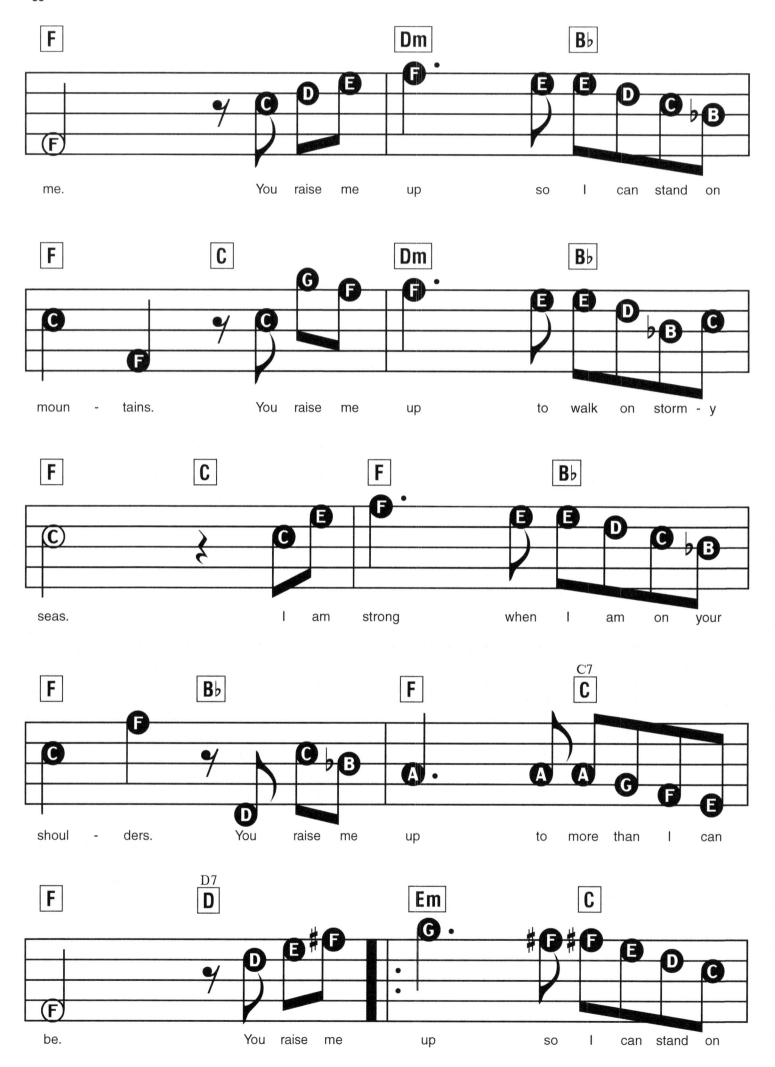

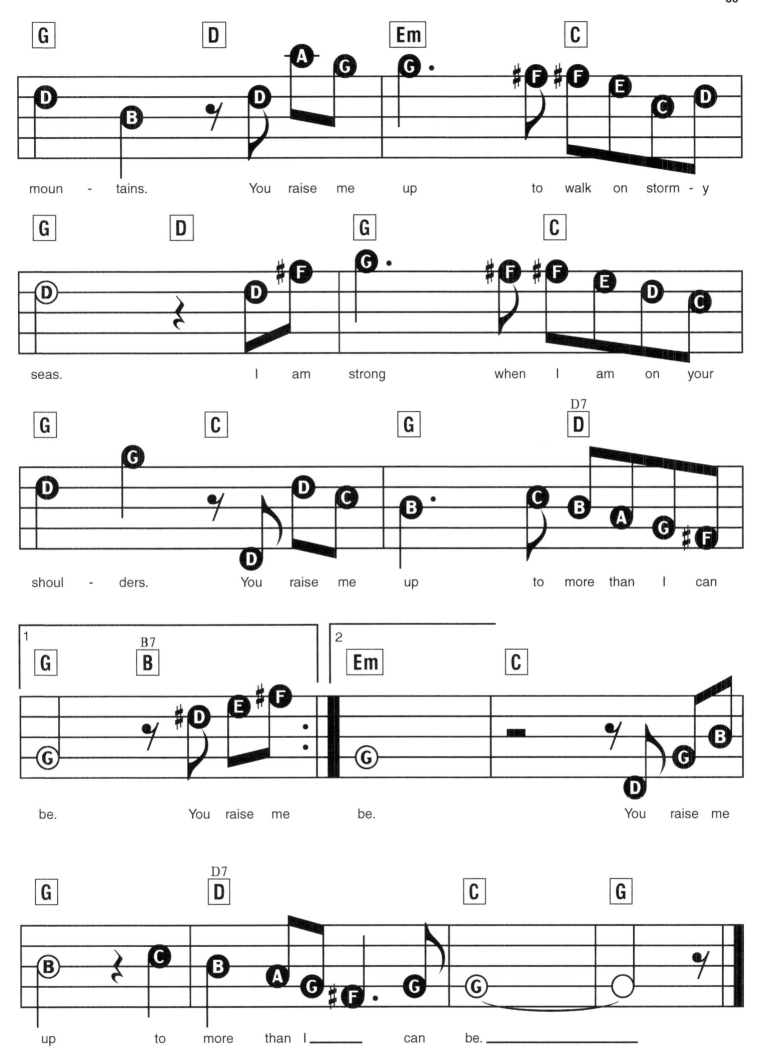

You'll Never Walk Alone
from CAROUSEL

Registration 5
Rhythm: Ballad

Lyrics by Oscar Hammerstein II
Music by Richard Rodgers

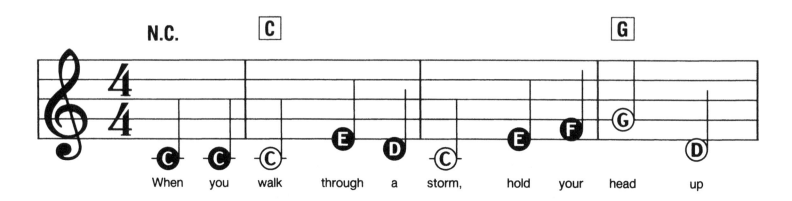

When you walk through a storm, hold your head up

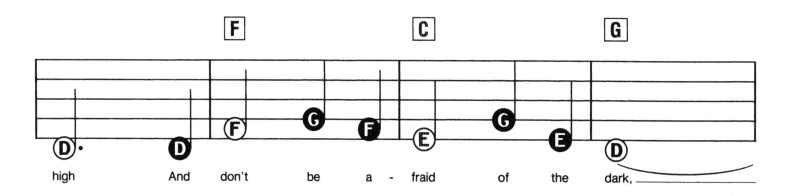

high And don't be a - fraid of the dark,

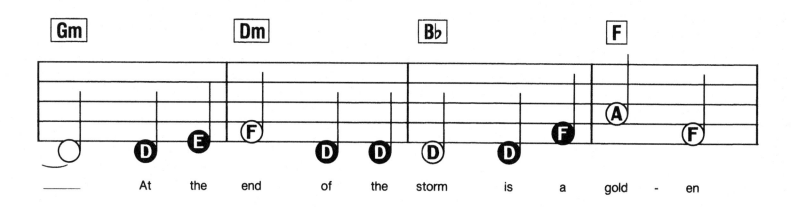

At the end of the storm is a gold - en

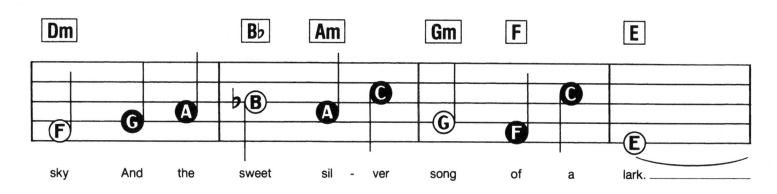

sky And the sweet sil - ver song of a lark.

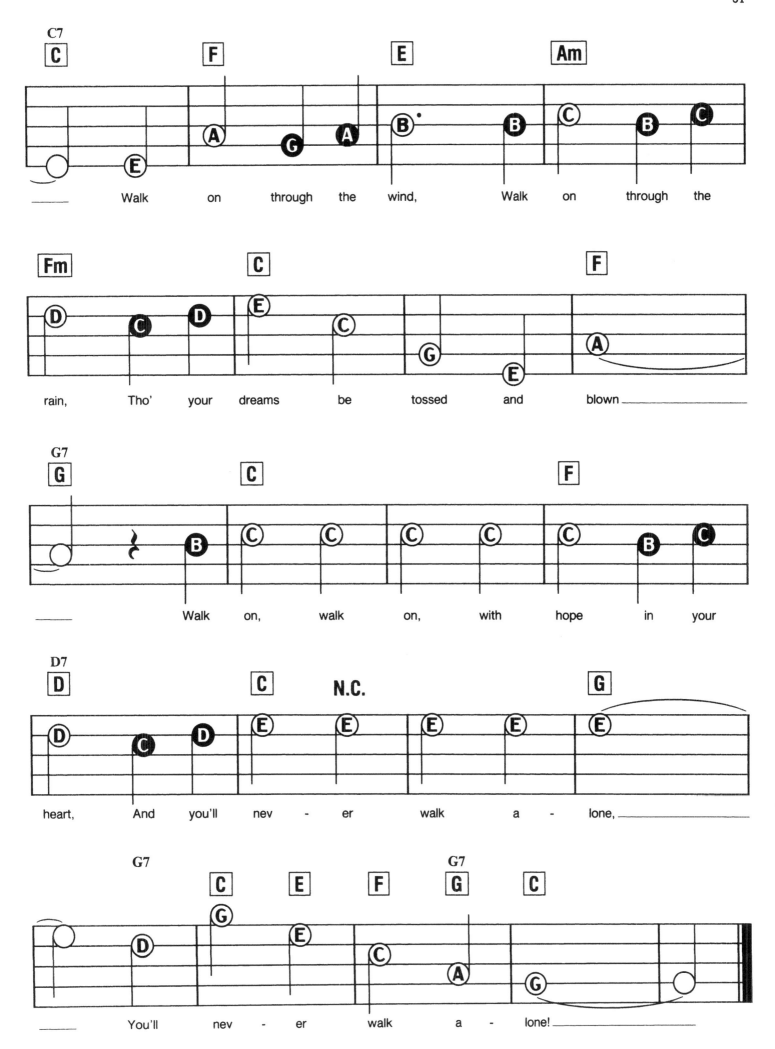

You've Got a Friend

Registration 3
Rhythm: Slow Rock or Ballad

Words and Music by
Carole King

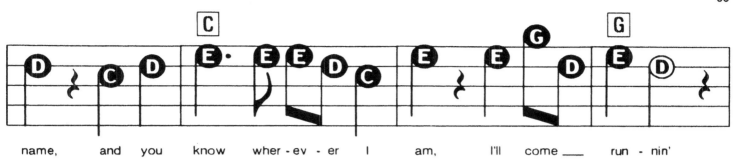

name,   and   you   know   wher - ev - er   I   am,   I'll   come ___ run - nin'

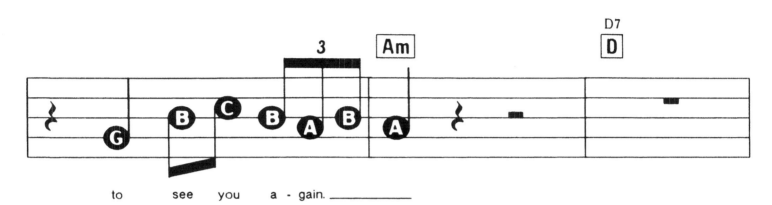

to   see   you   a - gain. _____

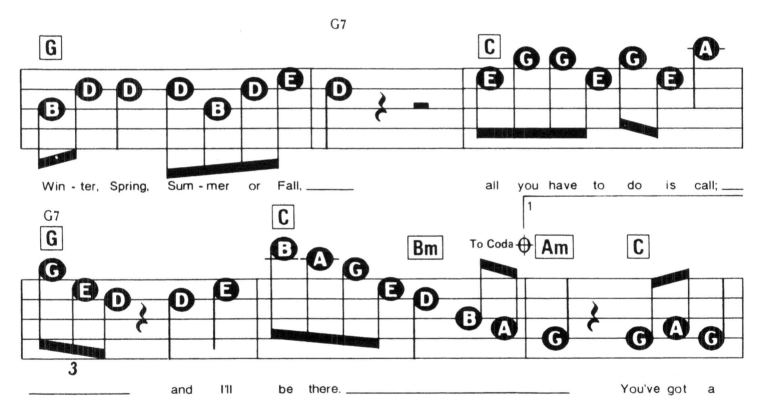

Win - ter, Spring, Sum - mer or Fall, _____   all   you   have   to   do   is   call; ___

_____   and   I'll   be   there. _____   You've   got   a

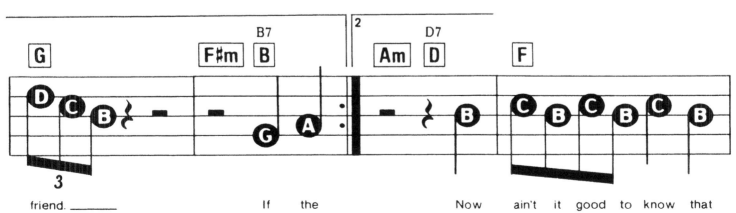

friend. _____   If   the   Now   ain't   it   good   to   know   that

94

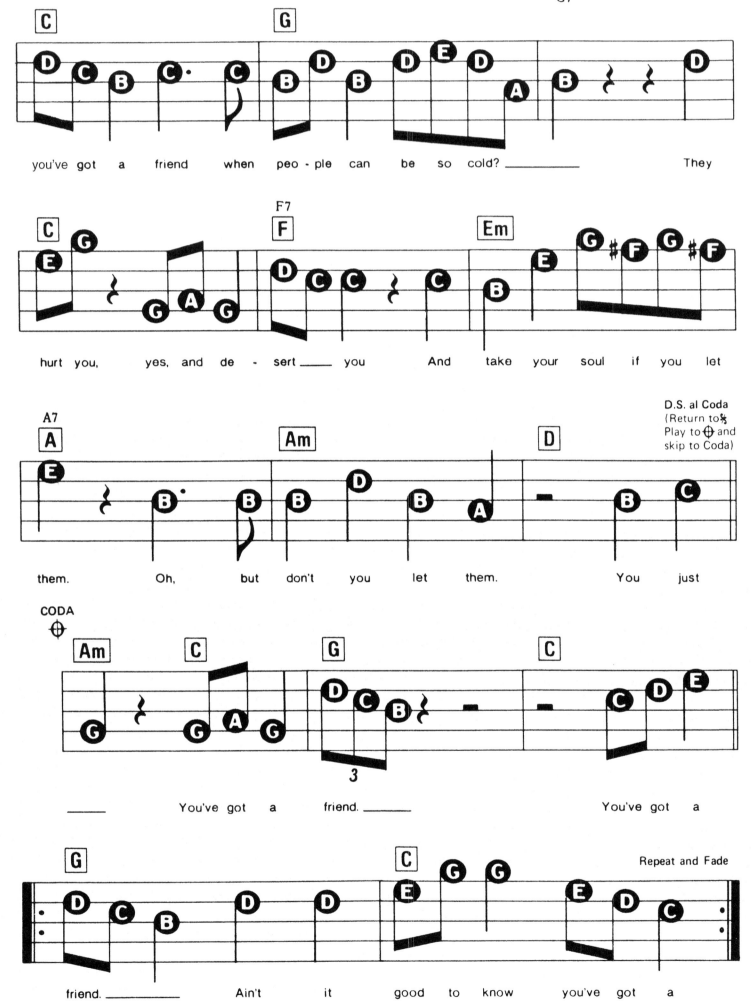

Registration Guide

- Match the Registration number on the song to the corresponding numbered category below. Select and activate an instrumental sound available on your instrument.

- Choose an automatic rhythm appropriate to the mood and style of the song. (Consult your Owner's Guide for proper operation of automatic rhythm features.)

- Adjust the tempo and volume controls to comfortable settings.

Registration

1	Mellow	Flutes, Clarinet, Oboe, Flugel Horn, Trombone, French Horn, Organ Flutes
2	Ensemble	Brass Section, Sax Section, Wind Ensemble, Full Organ, Theater Organ
3	Strings	Violin, Viola, Cello, Fiddle, String Ensemble, Pizzicato, Organ Strings
4	Guitars	Acoustic/Electric Guitars, Banjo, Mandolin, Dulcimer, Ukulele, Hawaiian Guitar
5	Mallets	Vibraphone, Marimba, Xylophone, Steel Drums, Bells, Celesta, Chimes
6	Liturgical	Pipe Organ, Hand Bells, Vocal Ensemble, Choir, Organ Flutes
7	Bright	Saxophones, Trumpet, Mute Trumpet, Synth Leads, Jazz/Gospel Organs
8	Piano	Piano, Electric Piano, Honky Tonk Piano, Harpsichord, Clavi
9	Novelty	Melodic Percussion, Wah Trumpet, Synth, Whistle, Kazoo, Perc. Organ
10	Bellows	Accordion, French Accordion, Mussette, Harmonica, Pump Organ, Bagpipes

00102278   1. Favorite Songs with 3 Chords $9.99
00100374   2. Country Sound $12.99
00284446   3. Contemporary Disney . $16.99
00100382   4. Dance Band Greats $7.95
00100305   5. All-Time Standards $10.99
00282553   6. Songs of the Beatles .. $14.99
00100442   7. Hits from Musicals $8.99
00100490   8. Patriotic Songs $8.99
00236235   9. Christmas Time $9.99
00198012   10. Songs of Hawaii $12.99
00137580   11. 75 Light Classical Songs . $19.99
00110284   12. Star Wars $10.99
00100248   13. 3-Chord Country Songs . $14.99
00100248   14. All-Time Requests $8.99
00241118   15. Simple Songs $14.99
00266435   16. Broadway's Best $12.99
00100415   17. Fireside Singalong $14.99
00149113   18. 30 Classical Masterworks . $8.99
00137780   19. Top Country Songs $12.99
00102277   20. Hymns $9.99
00197200   21. Good Ol' Gospel $12.99
00100570   22. Sacred Sounds $8.99
00234685   23. First 50 Songs You Should Play on Keyboard .. $16.99
00249679   24. Songs with 3 Chords ... $14.99
00140724   25. Happy Birthday to You & Other Great Songs ... $10.99
14041364   26. Bob Dylan $12.99
00001236   27. 60 of the Easiest to Play Songs with 3 Chords .. $9.99
00101598   28. 50 Classical Themes $9.99
00100135   29. Love Songs $9.99
00100030   30. Country Connection $12.99
00100010   31. Big Band Favorites $9.99
00249578   32. Songs with 4 Chords ... $14.99
00160720   33. Ragtime Classics $9.99
00100122   36. Good Ol' Songs $12.99
00100410   37. Favorite Latin Songs $8.99
00156394   38. Best of Adele $10.99
00159567   39. Best Children's Songs Ever $17.99
00119955   40. Coldplay $10.99
00287762   41. Bohemian Rhapsody $14.99
00100123   42. Baby Boomers Songbook . $10.99
00102135   44. Best of Willie Nelson .. $14.99
00100460   45. Love Ballads $8.99
00156236   46. 15 Chart Hits $12.99
00100007   47. Duke Ellington $8.95
00100343   48. Gospel Songs of Johnny Cash $9.99
00236314   49. Beauty and the Beast ... $12.99
00102114   50. Best of Patsy Cline $9.99
00100208   51. Essential Songs: 1950s . $17.99
00100209   52. Essential Songs: 1960s . $19.99
00348318   53. 100 Most Beautiful Christmas Songs $22.99
00199268   54. Acoustic Songs $12.99
00100342   55. Johnny Cash $12.99
00137703   56. Jersey Boys $12.99
00100118   57. More of the Best Songs Ever $19.99
00100285   58. Four-Chord Songs $10.99
00100353   59. Christmas Songs $10.99
00100304   60. Songs for All Occasions .. $16.99
00100409   62. Favorite Hymns $7.99
00278397   63. Classical Music $7.99
00100223   64. Wicked $12.99
00100217   65. Hymns with 3 Chords $8.99
00232258   66. La La Land $12.99
00100268   68. Pirates of the Caribbean . $12.99
00100449   69. It's Gospel $9.99
00100432   70. Gospel Greats $8.99
00236744   71. 21 Top Hits $12.99
00100117   72. Canciones Románticas .. $10.99
00237558   73. Michael Jackson $12.99
00147049   74. Over the Rainbow & 40 More Great Songs . $12.99
00100568   75. Sacred Moments $6.95
00100572   76. The Sound of Music $10.99

00238941   77. Andrew Lloyd Webber $12.99
00100530   78. Oklahoma! $6.95
00248709   79. Roadhouse Country $12.99
00100200   80. Essential Paul Anka $8.95
00100262   82. Big Book of Folk Pop Rock $14.99
00100584   83. Swingtime $7.95
00265416   84. Ed Sheeran $14.99
00100221   85. Cowboy Songs $7.95
00265488   86. Leonard Cohen $12.99
00100286   87. 50 Worship Standards .. $14.99
00100287   88. Glee $9.99
00100577   89. Songs for Children $9.99
00290104   90. Elton John Anthology ... $16.99
00100034   91. 30 Songs for a Better World $10.99
00100288   92. Michael Bublé Crazy Love . $10.99
00100036   93. Country Hits $12.99
00100219   95. Phantom of the Opera .. $12.99
00100263   96. Mamma Mia $10.99
00102317   97. Elvis Presley $14.99
00109768   98. Flower Power $16.99
00275360   99. The Greatest Showman .. $14.99
00282486   100. The New Standards $19.99
00100000   101. Annie $10.99
00286388   102. Dear Evan Hansen $12.99
00119237   103. Two-Chord Songs $9.99
00147057   104. Hallelujah & 40 More Great Songs . $14.99
00287417   105. River Flows in You & Other Beautiful Songs . $12.99
00139940   106. 20 Top Hits $14.99
00100256   107. The Best Praise & Worship Songs Ever ... $16.99
00100363   108. Classical Themes $7.99
00102232   109. Motown's Greatest Hits . $12.95
00101566   110. Neil Diamond Collection . $15.99
00100119   111. Season's Greetings $15.99
00101498   112. Best of the Beatles $21.99
00100134   113. Country Gospel USA $14.99
00100264   114. Pride and Prejudice $9.99
00101612   115. The Greatest Waltzes ... $9.99
00287931   116. A Star Is Born, La La Land, Greatest Showman & More . $19.99
00289026   117. Tony Bennett $14.99
00100136   118. 100 Kids' Songs $14.99
00139985   119. Blues $12.99
00100433   120. Bill & Gloria Gaither $14.95
00100333   121. Boogies, Blues & Rags .. $9.99
00100146   122. Songs for Praise & Worship $9.99
00100266   123. Pop Piano Hits $14.99
00101440   124. The Best of Alabama $7.95
00100001   125. The Great Big Book of Children's Songs $14.99
00101563   127. John Denver $12.99
00116947   128. John Williams $12.99
00140764   129. Campfire Songs $12.99
00116956   130. Taylor Swift Hits $10.99
00102318   131. Doo-Wop Songbook $12.99
00100258   132. Frank Sinatra: Christmas Collection .. $10.99
00100306   133. Carole King $12.99
00100226   134. AFI's Top 100 Movie Songs $24.95
00289978   135. Mary Poppins Returns . $10.99
00291475   136. Disney Fun Songs $14.99
00100144   137. Children's Movie Hits ... $9.99
00100038   138. Nostalgia Collection ... $16.99
00100289   139. Crooners $19.99
00101956   140. Best of George Strait ... $16.99
00294969   141. A Sentimental Christmas . $12.99
00300288   142. Aladdin $10.99
00101946   143. Songs of Paul McCartney . $8.99
00140768   144. Halloween $10.99
00100291   145. Traditional Gospel $9.99
00319452   146. The Lion King (2019) ... $10.99
00147061   147. Great Instrumentals $9.99
00100222   148. Italian Songs $9.99
00329569   149. Frozen 2 .... $10.99
00100152   151. Beach Boys Greatest Hits . $14.99

00101592   152. Fiddler on the Roof $9.99
00140981   153. 50 Great Songs $14.99
00100228   154. Walk the Line $8.95
00101549   155. Best of Billy Joel $12.99
00101769   158. Very Best of John Lennon . $12.99
00326434   159. Cats $10.99
00100315   160. Grammy Awards Record of the Year 1958-2011 . $19.99
00100293   161. Henry Mancini $10.99
00100049   162. Lounge Music $10.95
00100295   163. Very Best of the Rat Pack . $12.99
00277916   164. Best Christmas Songbook . $9.99
00101895   165. Rodgers & Hammerstein Songbook $10.99
00149300   166. The Best of Beethoven .. $8.99
00149736   167. The Best of Bach $8.99
00100148   169. Charlie Brown Christmas . $10.99
00100090   170. Kenny Rogers $12.99
00101537   171. Best of Elton John $9.99
00101796   172. The Music Man $9.99
00100321   173. Adele: 21 .... $12.99
00100229   175. Party Songs $14.99
00100149   176. Charlie Brown Collection . $9.99
00100019   177. I'll Be Seeing You $15.99
00102325   179. Love Songs of the Beatles . $14.99
00149881   180. The Best of Mozart $8.99
00101610   181. Great American Country Songbook $16.99
00001246   182. Amazing Grace $12.99
00450133   183. West Side Story $9.99
00290252   184. Merle Haggard $14.99
00100151   185. Carpenters $12.99
00101606   186. 40 Pop & Rock Song Classics $14.99
00100155   187. Ultimate Christmas $18.99
00102276   189. Irish Favorites $9.99
00100053   191. Jazz Love Songs $9.99
00123123   193. Bruno Mars $11.99
00124609   195. Opera Favorites $8.99
00101609   196. Best of George Gershwin . $14.99
00119857   199. Jumbo Songbook $24.99
00295070   200. Best Songs Ever $19.99
00101540   202. Best Country Songs Ever . $17.99
00101541   203. Best Broadway Songs Ever $19.99
00101542   204. Best Easy Listening Songs Ever $17.99
00284127   205. Best Love Songs Ever .. $17.99
00101570   209. Disney Christmas Favorites $9.99
00100059   210. '60s Pop Rock Hits $14.99
14041777   211. Big Book of Nursery Rhymes & Children's Songs $15.99
00126895   212. Frozen $9.99
00101546   213. Disney Classics $15.99
00101533   215. Best Christmas Songs Ever $22.99
00131100   216. Frank Sinatra Centennial Songbook . $19.99
00100040   217. Movie Ballads $9.99
00100156   219. Christmas Songs with Three Chords $9.99
00102190   221. Carly Simon Greatest Hits . $8.95
00102080   225. Lawrence Welk Songbook . $10.99
00283385   234. Disney Love Songs $12.99
00101581   235. Elvis Presley Anthology . $16.99
00100165   236. God Bless America & Other Songs for a Better Nation . $26.99
00290209   242. Les Misérables $10.95
00100158   243. Oldies! Oldies! Oldies! . $12.99
00100041   245. Simon & Garfunkel $10.99
00100267   246. Andrew Lloyd Webber Favorites $10.99
00100296   248. Love Songs of Elton John . $12.99
00102113   251. Phantom of the Opera .. $14.99
00100203   256. Very Best of Lionel Richie . $10.99
00100302   258. Four-Chord Worship $9.99
00286504   260. Mister Rogers' Songbook . $9.99
00100235   263. Grand Irish Songbook .. $19.95
00100063   266. Latin Hits $7.95
00100062   269. Love That Latin Beat $8.99
00101425   272. ABBA Gold Greatest Hits . $9.99
00100024   274. 150 of the Most Beautiful Songs Ever .. $22.99

00102248   275. Classical Hits $8.99
00100186   277. Stevie Wonder $10.99
00100227   278. 150 More of the Most Beautiful Songs Ever .. $24.99
00100236   279. Alan Jackson $20.99
00100237   280. Dolly Parton $10.99
00100238   281. Neil Young $12.99
00100239   282. Great American Songbook $19.95
00100068   283. Best Jazz Standards Ever . $15.95
00281046   284. Great American Songbook: The Singers $19.99
00100271   286. CMT's 100 Greatest Love Songs $24.99
00100244   287. Josh Groban $14.99
00102124   293. Movie Classics $10.99
00100303   295. Best of Michael Bublé .. $14.99
00100075   296. Best of Cole Porter $9.99
00102130   298. Beautiful Love Songs ... $9.99
00100077   299. The Vaudeville Songbook . $7.99
00259570   301. Kids' Songfest $12.99
00110416   302. More Kids' Songfest ... $12.99
00100275   305. Rod Stewart $12.99
00102147   306. Irving Berlin Collection . $16.99
00100276   307. Gospel Songs with 3 Chords $8.99
00100194   309. 3-Chord Rock 'n' Roll ... $9.99
02501515   312. Barbra Streisand $10.99
00100197   315. VH1's 100 Greatest Songs of Rock & Roll $19.95
00100234   316. E-Z Play® Today White Pages $27.99
00100277   325. Taylor Swift $10.99
00100249   328. French Songs $8.95
00100251   329. Antonio Carlos Jobim .. $7.99
00102275   330. The Nutcracker Suite ... $8.99
00100092   333. Great Gospel Favorites .. $8.99
00100273   336. Beautiful Ballads $19.99
00100278   338. The Best Hymns Ever .. $19.99
00100084   339. Grease Is Still the Word . $12.99
00100235   346. The Big Book of Christmas Songs $16.99
00100089   349. The Giant Book of Christmas Songs $9.95
00100087   354. The Mighty Big Book of Christmas Songs $12.95
00100088   355. Smoky Mountain Gospel Favorites $9.99
00100093   358. Gospel Songs of Hank Williams $7.95
00100095   359. 100 Years of Song $19.99
00100096   360. More 100 Years of Song . $19.95
00159568   362. Songs of the 1920s $19.99
00159569   363. Songs of the 1930s $19.99
00159570   364. Songs of the 1940s $19.99
00159571   365. Songs of the 1950s $19.99
00159572   366. Songs of the 1960s $19.99
00159573   367. Songs of the 1970s $19.99
00159574   368. Songs of the 1980s $19.99
00159575   369. Songs of the 1990s $19.99
00159576   370. Songs of the 2000s $19.99
00339094   370. Songs of the 2010s $19.99
00100103   375. Songs of Bacharach & David $9.99
00100107   392. Disney Favorites $19.99
00100108   393. Italian Favorites $9.99
00100111   394. Best Gospel Songs Ever . $19.99
00100115   400. Classical Masterpieces . $11.99